Practicing God's
Radical Forgiveness

Practicing God's Radical Forgiveness

Tracing the Practice of Forgiveness
in History, Scripture, and in Our Own Time

Jeffrey L. Bullock

CASCADE *Books* · Eugene, Oregon

PRACTICING GOD'S RADICAL FORGIVENESS
Tracing the Practice of Forgiveness in History, Scripture, and in Our Own Time

Cascade Books
An Imprint of Wipf and Stock Publishers
199 W. 8th Ave., Suite 3
Eugene, OR 97401

www.wipfandstock.com

PAPERBACK ISBN: 978-1-5326-4119-0
HARDCOVER ISBN: 978-1-5326-4120-6
EBOOK ISBN: 978-1-5326-4121-3

Cataloguing-in-Publication data:

Names: Bullock, Jeffrey L., author.
Title: Practicing God's radical forgiveness : tracing the practice of forgiveness in history, Scripture, and in our own time / Jeffrey L. Bullock.
Description: Eugene, OR: Cascade Books, 2018. Includes bibliographical references.
Identifiers: ISBN 978-1-5326-4119-0 (paperback) | ISBN 978-1-5326-4120-6 (hardcover) | ISBN 978-1-5326-4121-3 (ebook)
Subjects: LCSH: Forgiveness—Religious aspects—Christianity. | Reconciliation—Religious aspects—Christianity.
Classification: BT795 .B76 2018 (print) | BT795 (ebook)

Manufactured in the U.S.A.   JULY 21, 2018

DEDICATION

I would like to thank the many people who have supported me in writing this book, either directly or indirectly. Thank you to the parishes, diocesan members, colleagues, and family members who have taught me more about forgiving and being forgiven than they likely can imagine.

Particular thanks go to early, careful, and supportive readers, especially the Rev. Dean Gail Greenwell, Dr. Betsy Cook and author, blogger and advocate, Rebecca Tinsley. Your insights and encouragement were vital. Thank you to the Worker Sisters and Brothers of the Holy Spirit who invited me to direct a retreat on forgiveness. Their penetrating questions and support were invaluable in gathering all the elements of my thinking. Finally, I would like to thank my family, children and stepchildren, Meghan, Nick, John, David, and Kally, but most especially my wife, Kathy, for providing me with a harbor for forgiveness, healing, and faith.

"Then Peter came and said to him, 'Lord, if another member of the church sins against me, how often should I forgive? As many as seven times?'

Jesus said to him, 'Not seven times, but, I tell you, seventy-seven times.'"

Table of Contents

1

Questions, Questions, and More Questions about Forgiveness

No question, forgiveness makes a hot topic. Of course, you could say forgiveness has always been important, and that would be true. But forgiveness, like all human yearnings such, as family, marriage, and even love, has shifted and changed meaning throughout history. Think of marriage— marriage was at one time used to establish family bonds and seal diplomatic agreements, the kind of marriage long-ago King David practiced. In another era, the notion that any two persons would marry for love seemed absurd if not dangerous. See Romeo and Juliet for an example. The claim that two people can freely choose their partner would have seemed strange, threatening to the social fabric, even unimaginable as late as a century ago. This is still the case in some places around the world today. Forgiveness, like the other human longings, has also changed over time.

Today, the sense of what it means to be forgiven or to forgive has come to embrace personal redemption and the abolishment of resentments, a tool for reconciliation and community building, and more particularly, what forgiveness does for uniting God and humanity. Forgiveness, richly complex and nuanced, has grown from a simple settlement of differences to become, among other things, a tool for eliminating anger and strife. Forgiveness can free people of ugly resentments, resentments that burden our daily lives. And our understanding of forgiveness as a cornerstone of human and divine relations continues to shift and evolve. Forgiveness has come to embrace the breadth of our lives, covering far more than the resolution of a debt between two parties.

The church understands that the modern sense of forgiveness serves a fundamental pastoral need, not only of shedding resentments, but also of mending memories and establishing lasting bonds between the offended and the offenders. But more importantly, the church has come to understand that understanding the nature of God's forgiveness is a key to human flourishing. The peace that God offers through Christ and the Holy Spirit goes unmatched by any peace we can create for ourselves. Somehow, God, through forgiveness, wipes clean the slate of our history. We long to understand how.

Forgiveness has become a key tool for rebuilding relationships in the secular world. Irrespective of any church contribution, though often aided by the pattern of religious forgiveness, forgiveness has come to play a critical part in human actions as diverse as restoring peace and justice in South Africa, and recovering the rights and privileges of the Aboriginals in Australia. We need forgiveness, we desire forgiveness for others, and we long for a forgiving world. However complicated the practice of forgiveness has become, we need a reflective and inquiring look into its place in our lives.

I have corresponded about forgiveness with a friend of mine, Rebecca Tinsley, a journalist, author, and director of a foundation in Africa. Becky has been a witness to the outcome of the horror of the Rwandan conflict and has gone to lengths to bring remedy. She pointed out to me in an email an example of a murderer from the Rwandan conflict who not only did not seek forgiveness but in fact, pledged to do worse violence the next time. On the other hand, Becky wrote of a woman who saw her husband and children hacked to death before her eyes, and then was gang raped by the murderers, leaving her HIV positive. The victim forgave because that's what Christians are supposed to do.

Becky wrote to a Rwandan friend, Ariane, asking her views on forgiveness. I include Ariane's response as Becky, with Ariane's permission, shared it with me:

Dear Becky,

It is fine for you to ask. Yes, it is the case I forgave the people who killed my family because I did not want to keep anger. Mostly because I could not reverse things and have my people back. I like to face a situation or problem and get out of it. The killers did not ask

2

me for forgiveness. But I forgave them because I do not like to live in the past, I deal with a situation and life goes on.

There is a saying in Kinyarwanda which says "Uhombye Niwe Ubwimenyera." This means that "The one who losses [sic] takes the responsibility" I lost my family and I have responsibility for my life not the one who took them away. Also forgiveness cannot be taught, it is a gift given by God, no one can lead you to forgiveness except if given the gift by God. that is what I believe and how I have managed. God helped me directly.

The other point is that I put [a]way the past and live for the present and future. This helped to me forgive and move on.

With love,

Ariane

Ariane, now thirty-five, survived the Rwandan war—but not without terrible loss; both her parents and several siblings were murdered in the conflict. As you can read, Ariane has a powerful and nuanced take on forgiveness, combining several views of forgiveness into one response. Early in her letter, Ariane avows that she doesn't want to hold onto her anger. Her resentment will not change anything and the killers wouldn't ask for forgiveness in any case. She forgave because "I do not like to live in the past" and in that event, forgiveness provides a kind of therapy for the horror she experienced.

We should also note that Ariane talks about forgiveness from another vantage, not just the one-sided forgiveness of the victim seeking personal peace. She wrote that in her culture, Rwanda, the person who loses takes the responsibility for the loss. Ariane turns to her cultural roots to summon a kind of forgiveness that might be foreign to our Western understanding but remains true to her culture. Ariane believes a life well lived affords the best response to the murderers; they can violently take away Ariane's family but they cannot take away her dignity and her profound sense of responsibility. This kind of forgiveness, springing from her deeply rooted cultural understanding, shapes one kind of forgiveness Ariane practices even without needing to think about it. It's just what Rwandan people do.

Ariane witnesses to one more kind of forgiveness. She doesn't summon up sophisticated theological arguments or cite scholarship on the atonement. But she does speak with a profundity born of the simple encounter with God's gift of forgiveness. Ariane writes, "no one can lead you to forgiveness except if given the gift by God." Forgiveness as God's gift.

God alone can teach us what it means to truly forgive. Surely, we can forgive for other reasons, either to deal therapeutically with our memories and resentments or on the other hand to exercise the kind of forgiveness our culture teaches us to practice. But ultimately for Ariane, there's the summary forgiveness that only God can give. God, she writes, "helped me directly."

Ariane's remarkable letter, interweaving three different views of forgiveness into one understanding, provides me with a pattern for talking about forgiveness in modern life. She has witnessed and explicated forgiveness with a wisdom born of the terrible foundry of experience. As we journey through this book, please keep Ariane's weighty witness in mind for, as we all know, there's no greater understanding of forgiveness to be won than the understanding won by doing the hard work of forgiveness.

I set out to write a book on forgiveness intending to be probing and intelligent. I wanted to create a picture of forgiveness so compelling that in the end, the evidence for the healing power of divine and human forgiveness would be nearly incontestable. In many ways, I hope I didn't fail at that task. But I also discovered in the process of research and writing that claims made from the head, rational claims, would not persuade people. Emotions shape the work of forgiving even more than reason. In other words, we simply cannot think about forgiveness without talking about the powerful emotions surrounding the hard work of forgiveness. Forgiveness without emotion would not be forgiveness at all.

A friend questioned why I couldn't talk about forgiveness in rational terms alone. In every case where we see forgiveness at work, the first prompt to forgive begins in the heart and only then summons rational support from the head. We forgive and are forgiven either because we have a gut-wrenching desire to forgive or in turn, an equally powerful longing to be forgiven. Reasons to forgive *do* matter but true forgiveness begins in the heart.

We can test this with our own experience. Who among us has not lain awake in the early hours of the morning, tossing and turning, breast damp with sweat as we sort through the terrible things that we've either done or that have been done to us? Those chaotic memories, however painful they are, have been the engine of many fine works of art—novels and short stories, drama and films, even paintings. Perhaps it's the very discomfort, even the horror in reflecting on our past actions and sufferings, that provokes us to change. No doubt there are rational moments when we can weigh the cost of forgiveness, but it's not the rational thoughts that drive us to forgiveness. It's our powerful emotions. Emotions and intellect, mind and feelings combine to shape our hopes for forgiveness. Where shall we turn for a standard, a benchmark for forgiveness? I believe we must turn to God. I have an ambition for this book that by its conclusion, you will have come to value God's radical forgiveness as the formative force behind all forgiveness, both secular and ecclesial.

Some time ago, I was invited to speak by the Worker Sisters and Worker Brothers of the Holy Spirit (a lay and clerical order that works to serve outside the walls of the church).[1] One of the community members was a parishioner and she knew that I had spent a good deal of time studying and reflecting on forgiveness. Forgiveness was an important topic to the order's membership and appeared often in their conversations. The order wanted to know more and so we planned a three-day retreat.

Before we began the planning, I met with three of the sisters of the order. We spent much of our time talking about the nature of forgiveness and our feelings about forgiveness. Feelings mainly ruled the conversation. We four agreed that learning to forgive others or learning for ourselves what it means to be forgiven may be some of the most difficult work we do as human beings. Many people, we believed, long to shake off the bitter anger and frustration that surrounds someone unwilling to forgive. Still others find themselves filled with a gloomy sadness at some of the loathsome things we've done, wondering if anyone could ever forgive us. We agreed that we often wish for nothing more than to be forgiven and yet somehow absolute forgiveness eludes our grasp.

The three sisters helped me put together some questions to aid in planning the retreat, questions that continue to guide me. (You'll discover that when we discuss forgiveness, particularly considering Scripture, questions often outnumber answers!) Some of the questions were straightforward: How can we live with others who have hurt us, sometimes deeply injured us? How can we live with ourselves knowing some of the wrong, sometimes terrible wrong, we have done? These seemingly simple questions began to generate even more questions, all of them important in shaping our understanding of forgiveness. For example, if we forgive someone, does our forgiveness demand conditionally that the offender demonstrates a change of heart, or even more, experience a transformation, a conversion, of character? Does that mean we, the victims of the offense, the ones offering the

1. http://workersisters.org.

forgiveness, must change? Does forgiveness require the transformation of both the offender and the offended?

Questions like these generate even more questions, many equally important to understanding the nature of forgiveness. For example, if we forgive someone, who determines if the experience of forgiveness is lasting and complete? Does our forgiveness of an offender fall short and fail if we don't continually pay attention to our forgiving? On the other side, if the offender doesn't demonstrate lasting change, is the forgiveness only fleeting? We've all forgiven someone at one time or another only to have that person fall back into doing what first hurt others or us; does that mean that the forgiveness never succeeded, or that there is a "shelf life" for forgiveness? Could that mean that the forgiveness we once offered the offender was forfeit from the beginning? These are important questions not easily answered.

If you are a follower of Christ, as the Worker Sisters and Brothers are, the questions we have about forgiveness expand considerably. Some people recognize the idolatry, pride, and self-deceit that divide them from the Creator who loves them. The gloom of Job hangs over them and there's apparently no comfort to be found. How could God through the mystery of the cross forgive them? Those are the people I've asked leaving worship, following confession and absolution, if they believe they are forgiven. Almost to a person they answer with something like, "No, not completely." On the other hand, some people find themselves wondering what grave evil they could have done that would even require God's attention, let alone the cross. After all, isn't a good deal of my wrongdoing more a misstep or mistake, actions not to be taken too seriously?

When the beginning of the retreat arrived, I asked the sisters and brothers if they thought they knew what the word, *forgiveness*, means. As they responded I recorded their answers on a white board. Several people raised their hands and said that forgiveness was forgiving debts as in the Lord's Prayer. Several others said that we are to forgive and not forget. When I asked what that meant, they replied that we're to put hostility behind us, but at the same time we should never condone someone's angry acts or forget them. Nearly everyone thought that forgiveness was fundamental to the Christian life, and said that Jesus had taught us to forgive. Still others said that Jesus died to forgive our sins, though when those answers were probed, the people were not sure how death and forgiveness worked together. It soon became apparent that while everyone gathered often used the term *forgiveness*, there was no broad agreement to just exactly what forgiveness might mean and how we are to go about giving and receiving forgiveness.

The Worker Sisters and Brothers were better at theologizing than they thought. We collectively decided that we needed a working definition of forgiveness if we wanted to go on with the discussion. Together, they came up with an excellent definition: forgiveness takes place when someone who's been offended by another's actions deliberately relieves the offender of the weight of their offense. I think that's a thoughtful and penetrating definition; I believe the Worker Sisters and Brothers had summed up a simple common understanding of forgiveness.

Let's step back and look more closely at the definition. We hear three essential parts to forgiveness: that there must be an offender, the one who hurts another person. There must be a second aspect, the person or persons who were hurt, the offended. Third, and key to the whole notion of forgiveness, comes the deliberate effort on the part of the offended to relieve the offender of the weight of their actions.

I was happy with the Workers' theological efforts and I believe they were too. Working cooperatively, they had come up with a useful definition that was elegantly plain with three primary elements—two parties joined by an offense, and the relief of the debt incurred by the offender.

Definitions make for useful explanations. But just as a good dictionary explains meaning by quoting the word in its context, so too with good definitions of human emotions such as love, revenge, fear, courage, and of course, forgiveness; they need a context too. Do you remember the first time you told someone that you loved them? Very likely you didn't pledge your love by telling your beloved that every time you're in the presence your respirations increase, blood oxygen levels go up, and certain glands begin secreting complex hormones. Those are structural elements of love, if you will, but no one would mistake that pledge for love. More likely when you pledge your love, you'll share a narrative of your feelings. You will tell the person how they have moved your heart and soul, opened vast pools of feelings you didn't know you had, and brought you to a happiness you could never have expected. That's love!

Forgiveness has the same qualities—we need to offer a narrative of how forgiveness works if we really want to understand what we mean by "forgiveness." The early struggle of the Workers to come up with a universal and fundamental definition of forgiveness showed us something very important—not everyone understands forgiveness in the same manner.

As with so many formative concepts of our time, we soon discovered that there appears to be no timeless and universal definition of forgiveness, just as there appears to be no universal definition of key ideas such as love, marriage, justice, and compassion. No one definition rules. All definitions appear malleable. In fact, when we seek to understand forgiveness through narrative, we'll find that in the real world of forgiveness the definitions sometimes clash.

A lack of a fundamental definition shouldn't cause us despair. The narratives surrounding forgiveness are as various as the many voices of our culture. Some of them will be secular views of forgiveness, some of them religious, including Christian. In all the definition's rich variety, we can find stories about forgiveness that not only illuminate the views of those involved but from which we can learn as well. Some of the family members of the Emmanuel African Methodist Episcopal Church in Charlestown, South Carolina, killed by an avowed white supremacist, surprised the press. A few of the family members declared that they were prepared to forgive the murderer in their hearts; to be sure, they expected the racist, Dylan Roof, was to be tried and judged but then in some fashion forgiven.[2] The Emmanuel AME Church has a view of forgiveness that would be alien to many who believed that forgiveness of any kind should be set aside. The killer, the prosecutor believed, deserved the death penalty.

The Emmanuel AME example represents a contradictory view of forgiveness to some people. Emmanuel's sense of forgiveness, born out of a particularly rich cultural heritage, shows us how complex our ideas of modern forgiveness can be. Those of us who were not born out of Emmanuel's heritage might not grasp the internal logic of the members' forgiveness. We were raised with another narrative, another perspective, another understanding of forgiveness. Despite this complexity, there are still ways to go forward. In general terms, nearly all of us talk about forgiving and being forgiven. If we're not just self-deceived about the nature of forgiveness then when we forgive, *something* must be happening. Forgiveness is a practice, a habit of thinking and acting, formed for us before we were born. Whatever happens when we forgive, we know it best as we ourselves forgive or are forgiven.

The earnest work of forgiveness begins when we put our definition to work. Returning to the Worker Sisters and Brothers, our discussion opened the door to more questions. When we forgive someone, does that mean we

---

2. Merritt, "What Does It Take to Forgive Dylan Roof?"

should remember or forget the offense? Still others wanted to ask if forgiveness meant the same thing when we talked about forgiveness between individuals or between countries, or between minority and majority groups within a country? We live in a pluralistic world; countries and individuals alike suffer clashing values. We wondered aloud how we can forgive offenders, say terrorists, when they believe they're doing the right thing according to their ideology? Troubling though it may be to the victims, the terrorists believe they have the best interests of their families and nation in mind. How do we go about forgiving in such difficult circumstances?

Several people attending the Workers' retreat knew about the work of the South African Truth and Reconciliation Commission. Under Apartheid, many black South Africans were treated cruelly, tortured, and sometimes killed. Those South Africans who had survived to see the end of Apartheid recognized that lingering hate would divide the nation. How best should the country handle the unforgiving division? The Commission was organized to call on people to confess publically their actions under Apartheid. Because of those public confessions, in many cases, the offenders were pardoned. I believe there's no question that the Truth and Reconciliation Commission was one of the boldest experiments in forgiveness of all time. But questions remained in the hearts of some; was a confession by an offender enough to warrant forgiveness?

Other Workers wondered aloud about forgiving the dead, people such as spouses or parents, some of whom had been cruel to the victims. Can we forgive the parent or spouse who once wronged us even if we can no longer speak to them? Still others wanted to ask what it means to "forgive ourselves." If by our own definition we believe there must be both an offender and victim, what can be said of an individual who has been charged to "forgive themselves"? It's difficult to picture two identical people within one person at war with one another. Many were disposed to believe that learning to forgive yourself was key to personal growth in our time.

Near the end of the discussion, I asked what the Workers thought we meant when we said that Jesus died to forgive our sins. That was a hard question and one person said aloud in jest, "Hey, we didn't know we had done anything wrong!" Humorous though that jest was meant to be, to my mind no statement could be truer. As we progress through the beginning of the twenty-first century, we've entered a time when some people believe they couldn't have done anything worthy of the death of Jesus. In fact, if they had, they didn't know it! Plainly, thinking about the work of Jesus on the cross deserved more thought.

How then are we to think about forgiveness? Is forgiveness chiefly a tool for shedding our burdensome resentments so we may flourish as individuals, a view held by so many modern people? Is forgiveness but one step along the path to reconciliation at the personal, communal, or national level? We realized that while it's important to study and reflect on the work of forgiveness, in the end only the doing the actual work of forgiving or being forgiven fully illumines the meaning of forgiveness. While forgiveness may not be consciously front and center for us at any given time, we know that when we weigh up the things that matter in our life, the practice of forgiving and being forgiven counts among the most important elements of our memories. Memories of forgiving and being forgiven shape our entire remembered lives and with that shaping, also shape our future hopes. Forgiveness and forgiving impart vital meaning to our history and offer us purposeful direction for our future.

Whatever else may be said, it soon became apparent in our retreat discussions that we need forgiveness to forge new beginnings. Like all of you, I've had a great number of opportunities to reflect on my experience with forgiveness, either my own or my forgiving others. Too many chances, I sometimes feel! Reading about when Jesus told Peter that he expected us not just to forgive the seemingly generous seven times, but seventy-seven times, I feel as overwhelmed as Peter perhaps did.[3] I have had too many opportunities to forgive or be forgiven to count!

Perhaps you've had a similar experience to mine. You lie awake in the night, overwhelmed, burdened, psychically bruised and sleepless, thinking about forgiving. My memories of my offenses live again and again in vivid Technicolor and I know that without the relief of my forgiveness and being forgiving, they will continue. And those are just the offenses I have committed. What about the memories of offenses committed against me? How often do vengeful thoughts creep into our hearts when we remember past grievous offenses against us? You might think, "If I just had one more chance to take that person to task! I'd take care of them this time! I would make them pay!" Painful memories put a focus on both mine and others' offenses. Our own offenses sadden us and thoughts of revenge can be an unbearable weight.

Even if your memories of forgiving and forgiveness don't run to violence, all of us at one time or another are besieged by memories of needing to forgive others. Those memories launch a longing to forgive and

3. Matt 18:21–22 NRSV.

importantly, often at the same time, a feeling of an inability to do so. One of the fundamental truisms of modern secular forgiveness is that we need to forgive others if for no other reason than to shake off the enslaving shackles of our resentments. If you're a follower of Facebook, you know how often maxims like that appear. And yet, as soon as we utter that truism, that we need to forgive if only to be free ourselves, we must acknowledge that some aspects of forgiving others' offenses seem beyond our reach. How do we forgive the dead and the pain they have caused us? The great chasm of death lies between us and our offenders; how can forgiveness span that dismal canyon? How do we go about forgiving people the terrible harms they have done us, justified in their offense by their own minds? If you've been falsely accused, for example, how do you go about forgiving your accusers? What does that mean for forgiveness, especially for offenders who, self-justified, see no need for their own forgiveness? Add to that, what if the offending accusers have power over you? Many people strike out only to protect themselves; what can you do about forgiving people in that situation?

One concern dominates many other questions: how do we muster the courage, the compassion, the commitment to forgive even the most horrible of acts? Perhaps that can't be humanly accomplished. Some people, like the philosopher Hannah Arendt, reflecting on the Holocaust, believe some horrific acts are of such scale as to be impossible to forgive. Arendt believed that we cannot forgive the Holocaust because we cannot as humanity conceive of any punishment appropriate to the magnitude of the crime. We might naturally conclude that there are offenses that cannot be forgiven. Further, we might believe that there are some people who are beyond the reach of any kind of forgiveness. How shall we think about offenses like that?

Some years ago, I served a parish located in a conservative area of the country. Shortly after I arrived, terrorists struck the World Trade Center and several other buildings. The parish was in an enormous uproar, confused, as many were, about whether this represented the beginning of war or just what to expect. One parishioner had a distant family member who lost their life in the towers, compounding the church's pain at the event. Reactions were various. Several members wanted to parade the American flag on Sunday morning and still others wanted to talk about revenge. I am, as a Christian, opposed to violence and revenge, and so I sought to bring calm by offering a class on Islam, explaining why the terrorists were not representative of the whole. Over 250 people came. We talked about

Islam in general terms, but one fellow insisted we talk about the towers. What should America do in reply? What should we be doing? Angry and vengeful, he wanted answers, and I understood his feelings. But I asked him, if Christ had been on the top floor of one of the towers, watching the plane come for him, what do you think he would have said? The man, to his credit, took a deep breath and paused; he then answered, "Jesus would say, 'Father, forgive them for they know not what they do.'" Silence fell over the entire room. That's what Jesus would have said and we, all of us, declared followers of Christ, need to figure out if we would do the same.

If we go searching for resources to help us understand forgiveness, including secular, Christian, and divine, we'll soon find ourselves swimming in a turbulent, deep sea. Paul Hughes has written one of the best introductions to the topic of forgiveness in the *Stanford Encyclopedia of Philosophy*.[4] Hughes notes early in his essay that there's been a surge of interest in the topic of forgiveness over the past forty years and he goes on to make a broad and masterful summary of the various questions and issues that surround different approaches to forgiveness. Hughes's summary sentence to the entry tells us a great deal: "These and related queries will continue to draw the interest of philosophers to the topic of forgiveness, which *remains a complex, elusive, and contested moral phenomenon*" (italics mine). To put Hughes's remark in my own terms, despite all the work of philosophers, theologians, psychologists, historians, and more, we're still confused about what we mean when we utter the word *forgiveness*.

But again, that doesn't mean we should despair of understanding forgiveness. There are too many deeply felt memories and feelings about forgiveness to abandon seeking its meaning. Not too long ago, I dropped off some packages in a mail store to be delivered out of state. I had been there on several occasions in the past. I had shared with the woman who managed the mail store that I was working on some Christian writing projects and we had some lively conversations about writing, theology, and faith in general. She had volunteered that she had grown up in the faith (her father was close friends with one of the most celebrated of English philosophers) but now she had for the most part rejected her past spiritual practice. On this occasion, the mail manager asked me what I was working on today. I said, "Forgiveness." "Oh, my Lord" she said, hand to her brow, "I can't imagine anything more difficult!" I couldn't let an exclamation like that go. I asked her, "What do you mean?" "Oh," she said, shaking her head as if in

4. Hughes and Warmke, "Forgiveness."

pain, "I know I need to forgive. I know it!" "How so?" I asked. "Because," she said, "I was married to a real 'so-and-so' and I need to let it go." "Why don't you?" I asked. "If your memories trouble you that much, why not forgive him?" "Because I can't," she said, and with tears in her eyes, she added, "I know I need to but I just don't know how. And I just can't do it!"

That wasn't our last conversation on forgiveness but the mail manager's plight shows us something important—we can ramble and wonder about the meaning of forgiveness and how it works, but we need to come down somewhere. We need the experience of forgiveness, whether others or ours, and we need time to reflect on what forgiveness means. We need time to form an understanding of the practice of forgiving and forgiveness. To put it bluntly, if we are Christians, we especially need to come up with some meaningful way to talk about the gut-wrenching need to either forgive or be forgiven. I believe secular society needs helpful dialogue about forgiveness but to be more urgent, I believe we Christians need some answers, knowing that those answers likely won't be easy. We need as Christians to find a way to talk about forgiveness that brings hope and light to those in dark despair. If the cross was a gift of hope and light amid the darkness of death, then the cross must also figure in our understanding of forgiveness. Any church member can testify to their experience that there are enormous pastoral needs for those in need of forgiveness or who need to learn how to forgive. In an era where forgiveness has become a key topic of interest, Christians practicing forgiveness can become a powerful form of evangelism. If Christians are not about the business of forgiveness, what are they about?

Let's go back to Paul Hughes's remark about the thriving interest in forgiveness over the past forty years. Having read Hughes's statement, I thought I'd do a search on the topic of forgiveness on Amazon. I felt confident Hughes was well informed but when I plugged "forgiveness" into the Amazon search field, I was astounded at the result. More than thirteen thousand titles appeared! I would have liked to survey all thirteen thousand plus titles, but that wasn't possible. I did look over the summaries for the top hundred or so. Yes, there was no question, the topic of forgiveness had generated some broad and vigorous interest.

I soon discovered, most of those top one hundred sellers on forgiveness were devoted to what I think of as "therapeutic forgiveness." Just briefly for now, when I say "therapeutic forgiveness," I'm indicating a more commonly secular kind of forgiveness that best serves the individual who's been offended. The victims' need to forgive lies at the core. Cleansed by forgiving the offender, the offended can throw off the burden of past resentments. Therapy sets the individual free of the enslaving chains of resentment. Therapy sets right the illness or disorder that burdens the victim and while it's hardly a case of "just forget" the offender, the emphasis comes down fully on the psychological needs of the offended. If the weight of those injuries done to you burdens you so that you can compulsively focus on little else, "therapeutic forgiveness" can help.

Specifically, Christian forgiveness had fewer titles for pride of place. What can be said about the practice of Christian forgiveness? When we turn to the history of forgiveness (the 'history of forgiveness' exemplifies how the meaning of forgiveness has constantly changed usage over the centuries—it's meaning has been far from fixed or universal) we'll see how formative Scripture was in developing our understanding of forgiveness. We've arrived at the modern era and as with some other Christian disciplines, I'd contend that the Christian notion of forgiveness has fallen into disuse or even been rejected. Based on Scripture and church history, it's nearly impossible to talk about forgiveness without talking about the cross. For some people, even some Christians, the witness of the cross seems cruelly out of date; blood sacrifice and a tortured death hardly feel central to forgiveness in our time, and frankly to some, they are at odds with a gospel of love. Today there are many people who seek a means to forgive that agrees with their substantially individualistic views of psychology, rejecting any external authority such as the Christian tradition. On the other hand, I believe that the Christian tradition and the church have important things to say about forgiveness, including to the secular world. I believe that at the heart of Christian forgiveness lies the work of Christ in the cross and resurrection. Keeping in mind the work of Christ and the cross, let's turn now to what I call the "three strands of forgiveness."

2

The Three Strands of Forgiveness
for Our Era

THIRTEEN THOUSAND PUBLICATIONS! THIRTEEN thousand books, pamphlets, or journals on Amazon treat the topic of forgiveness in one way or another. How can there be that much to say! I don't think it takes any stretch of imagination to believe there are nearly as many approaches of how to think about forgiveness. You can sense from the diverse approaches to forgiveness how the struggles with forgiving and being forgiven remain a constant issue in every parish in which I've served.

I've served as a parish pastor for over thirty-five years. During that time, I have spoken about forgiveness to large church groups and small, individuals and fellow parishioners. By the penetrating questions I have been asked, I realize that there continues to be a great confusion about what it means to forgive and be forgiven. Three different approaches or issues began to surface for me over time. First, what forgiveness should mean to me as an individual. Second, what forgiveness should mean to me as part of our culture and more particularly, what does and should the church say about it. Finally, how forgiveness shapes the relationship between God and me. At first, these three approaches only became distinct upon reflection; at the time of the discussions, the issues were largely intertwined. But after some consideration, it has become clear to me that there are at least three discernible approaches with distinctive attributes critical to understanding forgiving and being forgiven.

These three approaches are not part of the ancient understanding of forgiveness; our most fundamental understandings of forgiveness turn out to be carefully tuned to the cultural context and period in history in which they are used. Nor do I expect that forgiveness will be approached in the same three ways in the distant future. If anything, given the history of how forgiveness has been understood, we can be assured that our picture will change. But for now, I see these three areas of forgiving and forgiveness governing our way of thinking about forgiveness. They are:

1. The personal and therapeutic sense of forgiveness.

2. The communal (or interpersonal) sense of forgiveness that's embedded in our culture and more particularly, how the church interrelates with that sense of forgiveness.

3. How forgiveness works in the relationship between God, me, and the world around us.

If I were to create a shorthand account of the three senses of forgiveness, I would say they are: 1. the personal, 2. the corporate and communal, and 3. the divine.

I have come to call these three senses of forgiveness personal, communal, and divine, the three strands of forgiveness, strands that woven together make up the rich complexity of modern forgiveness.

When people discuss forgiveness in practice, the three strands operate cooperatively to create the broader activity of forgiving. Rarely in my experience has anyone separated one from the other in discussion. In my reading and discussions, I've encountered these three strands, conjoined in practice but discussed as separate approaches. In discussion, I've found Strand One, the individual, concerns itself with the individual's psychic and spiritual well-being. Commonly, I've heard people express Strand One concerns most often about a victim shedding resentments that encumber him or her. Strand Two concerns the interpersonal relations of persons living in community, whether it be a family, church, or larger community. Most often talk of forgiveness in Strand Two centers on broken relationships and how they may be restored or reconciled. That's especially true within the church where tradition has long favored unity over division. Strand Three concerns itself with the relationship of forgiveness between the human and divine. In my experience, the Third Strand gets the least attention and yet to my mind, provides the single strongest cord comprising the three strands of the cable of forgiveness. There's a good deal of discussion about how to talk about God's forgiveness, but within the Christian tradition it's largely understood that Christ and the cross offer the sum of God's forgiveness. I would paraphrase the letter of First John, insisting that humanity could not learn to love without God first having loved us.[1] I would say the very same is true of forgiveness, that humanity could not know the power of forgiveness without first experiencing God's forgiveness. To my mind, eternal and radically complete forgiveness begins with God's act of forgiveness on the cross. That radical forgiveness forms the strong central strand that makes the three strands of forgiveness work.

I am not aware of any other person who thinks in terms of three identifiable strands comprising forgiveness; this notion springs from my own reflection and faith. I don't pretend that my view will enjoy intensive philosophical analysis or address questions of academic fitness; I'll leave that determination to others who have already made important contributions.[2] I think it would be nearly impossible given the current breadth of discussion about forgiveness to provide an exhaustive account of what forgiving and forgiven mean. I do believe that the time has come to deliver a clear approach to forgiveness for "people in the pews," for people who are working on becoming forgiven and forgiving people.

Returning to the Worker Sisters and Brothers retreat, I thank God that it came off well. I don't know how beneficial my work was for others, but I do know how beneficial the give and take, the questions and insights the group offered were for me. Every afternoon, after the day's presentations, I'd go back to my room and take notes on our discussion and questions about forgiveness.

Strand One, "therapeutic forgiveness," is the most common in our cultural today. I'll have more to say later about the definition of therapeutic forgiveness, but for the moment, the emphasis lies chiefly with the person exercising the forgiveness. People concerned with therapeutic forgiveness stress the cleansing power of the release of anger, depression, and resentment. All of us have suffered the insult of an offense, whether it be unkind words, an angry voice, or even a physically violent act, and the point of therapeutic forgiveness is to find a way forward to personal release, whether the perpetrator seeks forgiveness or not. No doubt people seeking therapeutic forgiveness wish for the offenders to own their offense, renounce it, take

---

1. 1 John 4:19

2. I have in mind the work of L. Gregory Jones, Fleming Rutledge, Desmond Tutu, and Miroslav Volf.

responsibility, and change. But even if the offender is unwilling or unable to do so, the one who suffers the offense can still forgive and be released from poisonous resentments.

I was surprised at the number of the Workers who were well versed in the practice of therapeutic forgiveness. One after another offered the common axiom, "Well, at least forgiveness is good for *us!*" In other words, while we may not be able to do anything about the perpetrator's response, we can, as an act of self-care, relieve ourselves of the burden of resentments. I agreed, forgiveness is at least good for *us*. I went on to point out scriptural resources for believing so but with a different emphasis. Whenever in the Gospels Jesus and his disciples spoke of forgiveness, Jesus always pointed first to forgiving the offender and then to the benefit for the offended. Rather than emphasizing the benefits for the one giving forgiveness, the Gospel emphasis falls on the one needing forgiveness.

Our discussion turned at that point from the individual to the larger community. The discussion led me to what I would come to call Strand Two, Christian forgiveness, especially as it functions in community. I urged the Workers to turn Matthew, chapter 18, which in its entirety is sometimes referred to as "the handbook of the early church." In verses 15–20, Jesus outlines a method for coping with sin among church members. There are steps. First, we should approach the sinner on our own as the one offended. If the sinner doesn't listen, then we should take two or three other church members with us to do the same. If after that, the sinner still doesn't listen, then we should take the issue to the entire church. Finally, if the third step doesn't work, we should shun the offender as a "Gentile and a tax collector." (I note here, though it isn't often remarked, that Matthew has often been referred to as a tax collector, making the resolution of shunning far from final. If a tax collector such as Matthew can become a Gospel writer, then shunning must be open to forgiveness.) Jesus goes on to say that whatever the church binds on earth will be bound in heaven, whatever the church looses on earth will be loosed in heaven. Jesus taught that the church as a community has the remarkable power to forgive sins, something about which we will have more to say later.

Following verse 20, we have a crucial exchange between Peter and Jesus on forgiveness. Having just heard the instructions Jesus has given regarding forgiveness in the church, Peter offers this: "Lord, if another member of the church sins against me, how often should I forgive? As many as seven times?" Jesus then responds to Peter, "Not seven times, but,

I tell you, seventy-seven times." We'll return to these important verses later but for the moment, let's focus on how magnanimously Peter wants to be regarded. Peter, longing to be recognized as an enthusiastic and completely sympathetic disciple, thinks he's taking the high road—should I forgive as many as seven times? If we look at Peter's assertion, you'll see that Peter's concern falls first on Peter—Peter is more concerned for the Lord's presumed admiration for his exercise of magnanimous forgiveness than he is concerned with those in need of forgiveness. When Jesus responds, we see that he shifts forgiveness from Peter's calculated response to an open-ended forgiveness. Let's reflect a moment on what Jesus offers: who can remember seventy-seven offenses as easily as say forty-two or one hundred and nine? We would think someone was mad if they compulsively counted offenses like that—even the faithful Peter. Jesus emphasizes forgiveness for the offender—offend and offend again, but whatever you do, we (Jesus and the church) assure you we desire to forgive. Peter may long to imitate what he perceives to be the Lord's magnanimity, but the reach of that magnanimity stretches beyond Peter's imagination. Peter's effort to calculate a hard number for the number of times we should forgive falls flat; the extravagant number Jesus offers is beyond calculation.

Some may argue that Strand Two is but a version of Strand One; surely the one forgiving in Strand Two will benefit from the relief of resentments. I would say certainly the ability to forgive will benefit Peter, the disciples, the members of the early church, and we too, members of the church today. But as we read earlier in Jesus' response to Peter, the emphasis in Strand Two falls chiefly on those needing forgiving and only after that, on the ones who are doing the forgiving. While much of what I say about Strand Two will be most relevant to the church, that's because the practice of Christians and the church are front and center for me. Strand Two applies to secular patterns of forgiveness as well; Strand Two, just as Christians do, seeks forgiveness for the benefit of those needing forgiving.

In 1994, in a period of roughly a hundred days, somewhere between five hundred thousand and a million Rwandans, a staggering number of human beings, largely Tutsi, were slaughtered in a genocidal conflict. Many Westerners had the mistaken idea that the Hutu-Tutsi conflict was a war between Islam and Christianity, but that was not the case. Both groups were nominally Christian and their respective tribes were among the earliest converts to Christianity. The conflict was chiefly about racism, and even that racism was, in the minds of some, a product of European insertion.

The conflict was racially motivated, not religiously motivated, but the steps to secular forgiveness between the Hutu and Tutsi were much the same as those of the church's—mutual recognition of the wrong done, repentance for those actions, and a change of heart and disposition. As we will see, the process of steps to Strand Two forgiveness for both Christian and secular are very much the same; it's the motivation that's different.

Let's talk about Christian and ecclesial forgiveness. The church seeks to be faithful to the ministry of Jesus by forgiving those in need of forgiveness, perhaps even forgiving the offenders without any desire on their part to be forgiven. That would appear nonsensical to participants in secular forgiveness; why would we initiate forgiveness if there were no mutual recognition of the offense? But the disciples of Christ, especially Peter, discovered that the impulse to forgiveness is preeminent in the life of Christ. So, it should also be with those of us who seek to imitate the Lord. The impulse to forgiveness on secular terms most often seeks reconciliation and peace; so too with the Christian impulse. In Strand Three, different from Strands One and Two, the impulse to forgive begins with God and works through the cross. God's forgiveness does not require that there be mutual recognition of the hurt that has been done. God forgives before humanity asks.

What then is the purpose of Strand Two forgiveness as it relates to Christians? When we practice Strand Two forgiveness, we recognize the communal nature of both the offense and the forgiveness. It may seem patently obvious to say this, but we must not forget that the original offense had to take place between two or more people. Strand Two forgiveness requires the underpinning of community even if the relationship between the offended and the offender is forged by hate. All Strand Two forgiveness springs from relationships and community that have run afoul. If communal peace is to be restored, then forgiveness must take place. Returning to the Hutu-Tutsi conflict, the Tutsi were latecomers, Bantu, who had moved into Rwanda. Encouraged by elements within Rwanda including European settlers, the Tutsi were often subject to abuse as a minority. This oppression benefitted the ethnic majority and forged a bond born of racism and hate. Intermarriage was not uncommon and Hutu and Tutsi lived side by side in some villages. Following the end of the genocide, perpetrators on both sides came to see how their relationships, however lopsided, were used against them. Strand Two forgiveness requires us to recognize those relationships and community.

Some might well wonder if the parallel between secular forgiveness and Christian forgiveness doesn't persist right through to reconciliation and peace. Peace for any reason makes a worthy goal. However, secular people may find themselves seeking peace simply as the absence of war. Peace born of secular forgiveness longs to open the door to prosperity and well-being even if only for a time. But the peace that Christians seek is an eternal peace, a peace like that of the relationship among the figures of the Trinity. Christians can rightly claim by faith that any peace that is not that of the communal three figures of the Trinity is but a parody of that eternal peace. Peace as an absence of war may be welcome for all sorts of good reasons, but anything short of Trinitarian peace remains but a poor imitation of the peace of the Trinity. No doubt some readers will view this eternal peace as unrealistic and unachievable. But Christians believe there is nothing more real than the Trinity, and therefore the peace that the three figures of the Trinity enjoy should and can be the peace that all creation enjoys. Much more could be said about the peace among the figures of the Trinity; their eternal peace and mutuality continues as the standard for peace among all creation.

Let's return to the communal character of Strand Two forgiveness. If we want to be empowered to forgive, we need to acknowledge ourselves as part of a community of forgiveness even if that community numbers as few as two persons. Two or more persons, two or more parties, two or more nations, however we make the count, the community always numbers at least two. If an injury requires one to suffer the injury and another to be forgiven, then the process of forgiveness must build on a community of at least two. The original hurt can be inflicted by a perpetrator for many reasons, spanning from regrettable accident to malevolent intent. Howsoever the nature of the injury, Strand Two forgiveness must by its nature always be pursued purposefully by both the offended and the offender. When we seek to practice Strand Two forgiveness, we seek the mutual effort of the entire community, including both the offended and the offender. In a strong sense, if the offended wants to forgive, we must have the commitment of at least the offended individual if not the entire community. In turn, the perpetrator must intentionally seek to right the wrong as Strand Two forgiveness requires both the perpetrator and victim working together. Victim and perpetrator must find a common language to talk about forgiveness, a common purpose and common intent.

Strand Two Christian forgiveness requires a similar commitment. Christians are empowered to forgive through a common spirit held together by a common language of faith, ritual, and Scripture. Seeking to imitate the fullness of Christ's forgiveness, we support one another, encouraging one another not to flag in our pursuit of Godly peace. No one of us in the moment may be able to summon the strength that is needed for Christian forgiveness, but with the aid of our fellow church members, we can be reminded, strengthened, and sustained for the taxing work of forgiveness.

What then of Strand Three? If Strand One focuses on the benefit of forgiveness for the individual, and Strand Two on the benefits to both the offender and the offended, what is the focus of Strand Three? The focus of Strand Three lies entirely on the Other. If you're not familiar with the expression "the Other," in theological and philosophical circles it has come to denote people who live outside of our sphere of culture. In plainest terms, the Other refers to anyone "not us," a "not us" that includes not our ethnicity, not our faith, not our culture, not our country, not me or us. The Other can be an acquaintance, a friend, or even a fierce enemy, but whatever the character of the Other, it is not me.

How then may we think of the forgiveness of Strand Three? As I conceive Strand Three, it's shaped by the forgiveness of the cross, the hard work of love that Jesus undertook in the crucifixion and resurrection. We can see Strand Three at work in Romans:

> For while we were still weak, at the right time Christ died for the ungodly. Indeed, rarely will anyone die for a righteous person—though perhaps for a good person someone might actually dare to die. But God proves his love for us in that while we still were sinners Christ died for us. Much more surely then, now that we have been justified by his blood, will we be saved through him from the wrath of God. For if while we were enemies, we were reconciled to God through the death of his Son, much more surely, having been reconciled, will we be saved by his life. But more than that, we even boast in God through our Lord Jesus Christ, through whom we have now received reconciliation."[3]

God's unexpected, uninvited, and perhaps for some people, unwelcome act of forgiveness underlies Strand Three. It's very important at this juncture to make something clear about Strand Three—Christ was not the adversary of humanity; humanity was the adversary of Christ. What does that mean?

3. Rom 5:6–10 NRSV.

For the moment, what that means is that Christ, through becoming fully human, emptied himself of every entitlement, and became just like us.[4] Christ reached across the gap that humanity had created with God, a gap created by breaking faith with the God who loves us, to become one with us in a new but imperishable relationship. Listen—we did not ask Christ to do this and in fact in our idolatry, we shunned God's past initiatives, the prophets and martyrs that had come before Christ. We as humanity had come to believe we had a better way of living on our own terms, a way that did not require God. In many ways, we were wholly unaware of our failings and self-deceived to think we were doing just fine on our human-made trajectory of success. But God, in God's sacrificial love, can never forsake us. And here's the most critical point of all: God has already forgiven us in Jesus Christ. That's it. *If you take nothing else away from this book, please take this, that Jesus Christ has already forgiven us. We didn't earn it, seek it, or even necessarily accept it, but God's forgiveness had already been given.*

I am not focusing on the notion of humanity's original sin; the Bible does not treat sin as an inheritable disease. Not one bit. Put original sin out of your mind. I urge you, considering God has already forgiven us, to see that the only offense we can offer God is the denial of God's love for us. How do we do that? Through idolatry. Many years ago, I heard a lecturer say that following the original idolatry in Genesis, everything in the Bible thereafter is a footnote to that idolatry. I'm not inclined to quibble. If you think about it, for what other reason would anyone reject the sacrificial love of God? There can only be one reason, that we believe we have a better offer, our love of self, our idolatry.

I see three strands of forgiveness at work in our contemporary world, all of them intertwined, all three essential to our life together. In simplest terms, Strand One focuses on my needs, Strand Two on the needs of the community, but the key strand, the one around which I believe the other two strands wrap, is Strand Three—the love of Christ for us from the cross, the love that dissolves once and for all the distance that lies between us and the love of God.

4. Phil 2.

3

History, Memory, and Forgiveness

PEOPLE ARE SOMETIMES LED to believe that the study of history is no more than a collecting of unchangeable facts about the past. If you too hold that view, I'm going to ask you to set aside that customary way of thinking about history, and consider with me history in a different sense. Let's think about the history of forgiveness from these vantages: how memory shapes and sometimes changes our recollection of an offense; how our understanding of forgiveness has shifted from classical times until today; and more particularly, how understanding of forgiveness has changed from Old Testament times until the time of Christ. In the latter, we will discover that the theme of idolatry extends throughout the arc of biblical forgiveness as we observe humanity first leaving God and then returning to a welcoming God.

Many think that the study of history works like this: we accumulate verifiable facts and gather them together in narrative form. Right? If you're an American, we believe we know US history from our time in school. We will have learned of George Washington, Ben Franklin, the "midnight ride of Paul Revere," and Abraham Lincoln. We will know the Civil War, World War I and World War II, and perhaps a bit about the Korean War and the Vietnam War. What we rarely see, and only occasionally acknowledge, is that for the most part that history lesson has been couched in a narrative of American ascendancy. Americans have been shaped by a curious mix of history and culture to think of themselves as entitled to success and growing continuously in accomplishment. Think about the history of the United States, and then how many American politicians in the past few decades have expressed the desire to recover a nostalgic picture of America. How can you argue with such a commendable idea? If you've gathered the facts as you know them, verified them as acceptable to you, and then told them in a narrative form, you could come up with a nostalgic picture that America was once filled with promise for every race and creed. But if you told American history in that way, you'd be leaving out some painful details. I don't think we need to scratch long at the nostalgic notion of America to see that the idea depends a good deal on who's telling the story. Could you imagine Native Americans or African Americans staking a claim to a rosy picture of the past? I doubt that the First People, the native Americans, would share the same narrative of history. Nor would African Americans, many of whose ancestors were brought into slavery, embrace a nostalgic view of American history. To these differing views of American nostalgia, we could add the unsettling development of labor laws and the trade unions in the nineteenth and twentieth century. If you had been a witness to the Triangle Shirtwaist Fire, when over 146 women and men lost their lives because of unsafe work conditions, you might be more reluctant to think simply and nostalgically of America history. Similarly, if you were descended as I am from Appalachian coal miners and pottery workers, you'd find it hard to overlook the terrible suffering of coal miners and their families in Matewan, Mingo Country, West Virginia, where they were suppressed by company goons. Elsewhere, we could reflect on the "white lung" suffered by pottery workers as symbols of an America that needs to recover its greatness. I bring up these sad moments in American history not to disparage America but to report them, to firmly remind us that history depends a great deal on how the story is told, who's telling the story, and most importantly to this author, how the events are remembered.

What do I mean, how remembered? Memories are memories, are they not? Discrete events and facts that are meant to be recollected from our past? We can't be faulted for thinking about memory in that fashion—for much of contemporary time, we have regarded memories as something we summon up from the "black box" of our mind, memories that are stored like data in a computer. Spin up our brains and the facts will be remembered. Or perhaps that's not how memory really work.

How Memories Work

How do we remember? We have come to recognize that memories aren't quite as concrete or substantial as we once conceived them. Conflicts about the verifiability of memory have arisen in the past years, including in the courtroom where eyewitness testimony no longer carries the weight it once did. Attorneys, judges, and legal scholars have found that even firsthand memories are dominated by context and perspective, and subject to change as time goes by. Think of the O. J. Simpson trial: time and again prosecutors found that passing time tainted not only the evidence but the memories of witnesses. Because of occurrences like that, scientists have been hard at work by various methods to uncover how memories work. CAT scans of the working brain and various other tests have shown the retention of memories to be far more fluid than once conceived.

Pixar released a marvelous movie entitled *Inside Out* that can help us understand the fluid nature of memories. The gist of the story concerns a young girl, Riley, who must move from her home in Minnesota to San Francisco. Naturally enough, the move raises all kinds of emotional conflicts for Riley. The movie focuses in large part on what happens in Riley's mind, particularly with her emotions, Joy, Fear, Anger, Disgust, and Sadness. Riley's mind, conceived metaphorically by Pixar as a control center, amply demonstrates something important about memories—emotions play a big part in how our memories are retrieved and how they're shaped. The movie based its interpretation of memory on the research of Dacher Keltner and Paul Ekman.[1] Over the course of the movie, Riley's memories change by the force of her emotions, changes symbolized in the movie by changing colors. What else could blue represent? Memories shaped by a particular emotion gain that emotion's coloring. The changed memories shift Riley's current perception of her life. The narrative of the movie forms a strong visual reminder that emotions can change over time, and that those changing emotions can change memories.

When we apply what we have learned from Riley's memories to the topic of history and forgiveness we can draw some important conclusions. The fact that emotions and memories can change points out that we can and do have a changing perception of a remembered offense, regardless of whether we are the offended or the offender. Even our memory remains malleable. Think about what happens to your memory of an offense as you come to understand the offender's social context. If you find over time that the offender suffers from say, mental illness and alcoholism, some of the

1. Ekman conceived of there being six emotions, the five above and "surprise," but Pete Doctor, the author and director, thought surprise too close to fear. See Cavna, "Inside the mind of 'Inside Out.'"

what if you don't know?

bitterness of the recalled offense will likely melt away. Your sorrow for the offender's plight can do a great deal to ameliorate your own suffering.

I once sat on a panel discussion of forgiveness as it applies to juvenile crime, family violence, and murder. One of the panelists had been charged with the responsibility for what the city calls "Restorative Justice," an effort to reconcile victims and offenders. The panelist told of an encounter where she urged the victim to see that the offender comes from a broken home in a rough section of the city. She asked the victim, wouldn't you be disposed, having discovered that to be the case, to feel differently about the nature of the offenses? The victim agreed. If we thought of offenses as fixed and implacable "facts," we'd have no grounds to change our minds. But once we introduce the notion of memories being shaped by emotions, we recognize that the history of forgiveness must be fluid as well.

Many years ago I spent a summer as a chaplain-in-training in a California prison. One of the inmates was among the most notorious criminals in American history, both feared and reviled. I had occasion to read his "jacket," the manila file including the history of his childhood. I was appalled at his background; driven from orphanage to institution and back again, often abused, sometimes sexually, his history was a horror story. I had no sympathy for his crimes but I did come to understand that his circumstances had deeply influenced him. My memories of his crimes were shaded by my awareness of the history of his abuse.

Adam Gopnik reflected in *The New Yorker*[2] on the mutability of memories. He wrote, "One might expect the rule of the past to be simple: that memorable things get remembered. But, in truth, what gets remembered is usually stranger and much more haphazardly stored. Many things worth remembering vanish; some things that you would expect to vanish remain." Gopnik continued:

> The better question may be what divides our past so radically between the things we remember and the things we don't. It may be that the general force of anxiety that affects everything in modern life is also responsible for the way our pasts get divided. The truth about modern life is that it creates enormous anxiety at every moment. It's like a traumatic force that suppresses some memories and refuses to suppress others at all. Our past is divided between the archival and the available exactly because it is so quickly past— so rapidly dissolved in confusion. *We all want to stop the process of traumatic change from happening, and sometimes we do it by*

2. Gopnik, "Why We Remember the Beatles and Forget So Much Else."

forgetting everything, sometimes by remembering almost too much."
(Italics mine.)

As Gopnik points out, whether we call our memories confused or not, it becomes readily clear that as we grapple with the nature of forgiveness, even the nature of the offense can and will change in our memories. And equally we recognize how, if we are the offended, our memories shift and change about the nature of the offense.

Gopnik draws the same conclusions that director Pete Doctor did for *Inside Out*—our memories suffer from a "traumatic force" born of the terrific anxiety of modern life. Gopnik continues by pointing out how selective our memories really are, that we archive and forget, sometimes to the end that we forget everything or remember too much. An offense remembered, whether by the offended or the offender, renders as fluid and alterable.

Miroslav Volf, a well-known theologian, has given the nature of memories, and especially memories particular to Christians, a great deal of thought. Not long ago, he engaged in an interview with philosopher James K. A. Smith, where the two reviewed the substantial points of how Volf views memories and particularly those memories that contribute to forgiveness.[3] Early in the interview, Volf criticizes the shortcomings of nostalgia and memory, shortcomings he believes contribute to forgetting injustices, chiefly our own. One of Volf's emphases in his book *The End of Memory* is that we must engage in "truthful" remembering. Because of forces like nostalgia, our memories (as Gopnik notes above) tend to corruption, ignoring our complicity in injustice and in the work of forgiveness. Volf said, "every untruthful memory is an unjust memory, especially when it concerns relationships, fraught relationships of violence between people." Volf asserts that all our memories are essentially "pragmatic," in that we do something with our memories (or they would not be memories at all). We remember and act on our remembering, not separately but as one action. What does that mean? That the very act of remembering is indeed just that, an action, and that as we saw with Riley how emotions shape memories, so too with the act of remembering. Emotions shape the very act of remembering. Consider how and when we remember insults to us. If I recollect an injury done to me amid other stresses I'm suffering, I'll likely remember that injury with great ill will. The circumstances surrounding the injury will have less effect on me than the angry act of remembering. One of the ways modern people cope with memories is through psychotherapy. Let's

3. Smith, "The Justice of Memory, the Grace of Forgetting."

take that previous memory and have it recollected during a therapy session. One of the tools that therapists keep at their disposal is "reframing," that is, to take a memory of a hurt and reframe it to illuminate the memory for different contexts, understanding, and history. The therapist might well ask, "Now that you remember your former friend's illness, their suffering with bipolar illness and alcoholism, don't you see what they did in a different light?" You would have to have a heart of stone to say "No." So remembering truthfully, as Volf speaks of it, may require our overcoming some personal but problematic idea of injustice.

When we talk about truth, we tend to believe that somewhere, somehow, there's a foundational truth that we can finally discover beneath our fluid and corruptible memories. Volf argues against this view; there's no foundational platform that finally says "This is the final truth" about our memories. How then do we discover the truth about even our own memories? How do we know which memories are "truthful" and which are not? Volf says: "I see the memory of the cross as the regulative 'meta' memory that situates all of our remembering and shapes it." In other words, the memory of the cross becomes a unique, super memory that provides an unfailing memory against which all other memories may be measured. Volf's point makes for critical importance to how Christians remember their history, especially the history of forgiveness. For Christians, if there can be an eternal measure by which we remember truthfulness, then it must be by the cross and resurrection of Christ. The cross and resurrection, marking the hinge of history, remains for Christians the only immutable event. In fact, I'd agree with Volf that we simply have no other standard by which to assess truthfulness than the verity of the cross and resurrection. We, as Christians, believe that the cross and resurrection lie at the very center of time; everything about our history comes measured from either prior to the cross or following it. For Christians, the cross changed everything, everything about history and everything about human hope—and our human memories. Our memories can be colored and recolored many times by our emotions, or the reframing of our memories. But the core of all our memories as Christians must lie in the remembering of the cross and resurrection. If there's no other foundational platform for our memories, we have the foundational truth of Jesus Christ raised from the dead.[4]

4. I once heard a theologian, Stanley Hauerwas, respond to the notion that "9/11 had changed everything forever," by saying, "No, everything changed once and for all in 33 CE by the cross and resurrection."

Just exactly how does Volf think this truth guides our own memories? The memory of the cross and resurrection causes us to remember our own wrongs weighed against the gift of goodness in the resurrection. Volf said, "I've got to remember what I did and wrongs that I did so as to be able to purify my own sense of who I am and my history, no matter what the other person does." Whether the other person in our relationship of forgiveness remembers just as truthfully is of course important, but we can only hope that our own commitment to Christian truthfulness will shape their minds as well.

Recognizing that the other person in a relationship of forgiving and forgiveness may not see things the same way we do brings up the question of forgetting. What if the other party forgets what happened? What if we forget, as Gopnik suggested, perhaps in our anxiety? Even more strongly, we must wonder about the oft said maxim, "I can forgive but never forget!" Most of the practitioners of the First Strand of forgiveness (and some in the Second Strand) own that maxim.

Treating memories as fixed and immutable facts raises problems for our forgiving. In the First Strand (and sometimes in the Second Strand) of forgiveness, the remembering of an offense becomes indispensable—it's the memory alone that protects us against the offense happening once again. If we're in a relationship with a practicing alcoholic, we can let our memories lapse for several reasons, including that it seems easier not to resist. But forgetting the offense of the alcoholic only encourages more drinking and discourages lasting change. More than just a defense, memory becomes in fact the cornerstone of justice—if we do not remember what happened, the unjust act can happen again and again. Without the proper memory of the offense, we have no means by which to hold the offender accountable! Liars within the cultural and psychological context of the First Strand won't change their psychology without being held accountable. Forgetting will undermine the efforts of Strand Two forgiveness; remembering acts as a bridge between offender and victim.

Volf insists, however, that irrespective of the claims of psychology, that we can forget, indeed we as Christians must and will forget. In an intriguing turn, Volf begins by telling Smith that many people might well be offended if forgiveness were demanded from victims. Somehow, that seems like piling on more responsibility on someone who has already been victimized. But Volf responds to that objection: "My response is: strangely enough, victims often want to forgive. They do so partly because forgiveness is a power act in the sense that they assert themselves as moral agents who are in the right and hold, in a sense, the moral status of the perpetrator in their own hand, even by the very act of releasing that person from the just demands of justice." Volf makes an extraordinary claim—some people want to forgive, not just to relieve themselves of the burden of resentments, but also because forgiving would elevate not only the moral status of the one forgiving but also quite possibly the forgiven.

What can we make of this? For the moment, Volf's appears to be leaning towards what I would call "absolute" or "unconditional forgiveness." In other words, the victim forgives chiefly for the benefit of the perpetrator. We will discover that when the forgiver, God, in the Third Strand forgives, God doesn't forgive for God's own benefit—God's self-evidently constitutes the highest moral status. God doesn't need forgiveness. Surprisingly, in comparison to Strands One and Two, forgiveness in the Third Strand strictly benefits the Other, and that benefit comes entirely without strings attached.

Volf's argument for forgetting may seem contrary to logic. But you may grasp the course Volf pursues by seeing that he claims that in the eschaton, at the end of time, in the final judgment of humanity, everything will be forgotten by God. Absolutely everything. Most people hear the term *judgment* in modern times and naturally assume the pejorative. Judgment signifies for many moderns that we have been judged and have been found wanting; none of us seemingly would welcome that kind of judgment. Not Volf, however. Instead, he sees in God what Volf calls "loving remembering." In this remembering born of love, God remembers only who we are and for what we were created. Sins and misdeeds no longer matter. Our faults fall away finally forgiven *and* forgotten. In this forgiven state, God establishes the eternal kingdom of peace, a kingdom where "loving memory" serves to unite all of us, the offended and the offender. In this act of "loving memory," our complete forgiveness was granted to us by God in Jesus Christ by the cross and resurrection.

Volf's picture of forgiveness takes the breath away in the breadth of its assumption—our forgiveness becomes an absolute, no strings attached, unconditional gift from God. If this idea of unconditional forgiveness troubles you, please consider this: if God created everything, including time, cannot God not only remember but more importantly in the resurrection, forget? Of course, God can. Our memories of an injury may be long but God's power of forgetting is longer. As Volf noted above, as we understand the

First and Second Strand, if we focus only on justice and conversion, we may miss the greatest gift of all, the gift of absolute forgiveness. Do we already know this forgiveness? Only in a mirror dimly, as Paul might say.[5] We have intimations of absolute forgiveness in all sorts of relationships; I can't count the number of times I've been unconditionally forgiven by my dogs, let alone parents, spouse, and friends! In the resurrection from the dead, all of what we are will be fully known and in that fullness, forgiven and our sins forgotten. Christ gave us this unconditional forgiveness and while it may not depend on whether we are Christians or not (see Matthew 28), we who know this extraordinary gift of forgiveness have also been given extraordinary lives.

5. "For now we see in a mirror, dimly, but then we will see face to face. Now I know only in part; then I will know fully, even as I have been fully known." (1 Cor 13:12 NRSV)

4

The Shifting History of Forgiveness

FORGIVENESS IS FORGIVENESS IS forgiveness, wouldn't you think? When we examined forgiveness as we have considered history and memories, we recognized that memories are malleable. Memories are shaped and formed by our emotions. It follows that even though we may remember a hurt inflicted on us, as time goes by we may remember the nature of the hurt quite differently. If the memory of the injury can change, doesn't that mean too that the nature of forgiveness can change? Is forgiveness malleable as well? Our fundamental question might be, does forgiveness mean the same in all places and at all times? When we read about forgiveness in the Bible, Old and New Testament, are we not reading about the same forgiveness we practice today? As we will see, apparently not. One of the rich gifts of the twentieth and twenty-first centuries has been the growing realization that many of the notions we cherish—such as love, honor, courage, and yes, forgiveness—have a history. All of them are historically conditioned not only by the passage of time but by circumstances as well. If we want to fully understand the richness of our modern understanding of forgiveness, we must consider how forgiveness has been understood in history.

David Konstan has written a truly remarkable book, *Before Forgiveness: The Origins of a Moral Idea*. The book that will be our guide for our upcoming discussion. Konstan, a classics scholar, searched through history, classical, biblical, and modern, to discover how forgiveness has been understood in different times and different cultures. His insightful discoveries can help us better understand how we've come to practice forgiveness in all three strands.

Konstan begins his book with this declaration:

33

"The thesis of this book is easily stated: I argue that the modern concept of forgiveness, in the full and rich sense of the term, did not exist in classical antiquity . . . [and] that it played no role whatever in the ethical thinking of those societies." More, the full modern sense of forgiveness "is not fully present in the Hebrew Bible, nor again in the New Testament." Konstan concludes that "it would still be centuries—many centuries—before the idea of interpersonal forgiveness, and the set of values and attitudes that necessarily accompany and help define it, would emerge."[1]

To restate in brief Konstan's view, nowhere in Greek or Roman cultures, Old or New Testaments, do we find the complex view of forgiveness that we hold today. That doesn't mean that there were times when people didn't practice forgiveness, but it does mean that when people of another age spoke or wrote of forgiveness, they meant something significantly different from what we think of as forgiveness.

We should take a moment to clarify what Konstan means by the rich sense of modern forgiveness. When Konstan speaks of modern forgiveness, he has three key points in mind. Konstan has the sense that between two people, the offended and the offender, develops a dialogue around confession—that is that the two agree about the wrong committed. If the offended forgives the offender, repentance follows and consequently a change of heart for the offender as well. Konstan points out that these three points are largely if not completely nonexistent in classical accounts of forgiveness. He even concludes (though I do not fully agree with him) that much the same is true in the Bible. Quoting the philosopher Charles Griswold, Konstan writes: "To forgive someone . . . assumes their responsibility for the wrongdoing," and it occurs in a context in which the wrongdoer and wronged party accept "the fact that wrong was indeed done, and done (in some sense) voluntarily."[2]

How then is modern forgiveness different from classic forgiveness? Evidently classic forgiveness largely involved settling a debt, though it could include a setting right of an inadvertent wrong performed by the offender. We have echoes of this ancient sense of forgiveness in our modern forgiveness, especially when it comes to jurisprudence. Once the appropriate debt is paid, everything is resolved between the offended and the offender. Notably, unlike modern forgiveness, the offended expects no change of character to follow. The debt is resolved; the forgiveness continues without

1. Konstan, *Before Forgiveness*, location 53.
2. Konstan, *Before Forgiveness*, location 165.

further reflection. The wronged in the classical world likely never expected a change of heart or of character on the part of the wrongdoer.

Konstan believes that the modern concept of forgiveness developed as our understanding of the individual changed. In the last 200 years, we've come to strongly emphasize the central importance of the individual. Our picture of society, whether true or false, conceives of society as largely composed of voluntary associations among discrete individuals and, unlike in the classical world, the modern individual operates largely autonomously. As we consider Strands One and Two, forgiveness on modern terms requires us to think in terms of individual transformation, psychologically and perhaps culturally as well. In other words, we have come to believe that we can will ourselves to be different people, and that the ability for the self to be transformed, requires that the wrongdoer undergo the same. If the wrongdoer doesn't have a change of heart, then that indicates that the wrongdoer doesn't truly repent of their wrongdoing.

We will return to this definition in later chapters, but as you perhaps already see, there are holes in such a view of forgiveness that should be considered. We must wonder to ourselves, "What happens when our understanding of what constitutes a wrong has been reshaped?" Perhaps what in the past was considered an offense has become a virtue. In the classical world, patience was considered a fault, if considered at all; in the modern world, patience is counted as a virtue.[3] Only an extremist contemporary Christian still believes as the Crusaders did that cleaving the enemy's head with an ax is an act of faith. Similarly, we must wonder just over what length of time a wrongdoer must acknowledge their fault? If the offender in time forgets their acknowledgment of the offense, ignoring that they once committed to a change of character, does that mean no forgiveness ever took place? These and similar questions comprise many of the issues surrounding Strand One forgiveness and a fair share of Strand Two forgiveness as well.

Compare our discussion of the elements of modern forgiveness to the resolution of a debt following a wrongdoing (the accidental killing of livestock, a cow for example) in the classical world. In the Greek and Roman world, to set things right we would repay the cow with another cow or something of equal value. At that point, forgiveness has been accomplished. But by comparison, not so in the modern world. Let's say you have inadvertently killed my pet while driving your car. If you have killed my pet,

---

3. See my book, *Practicing Christian Patience.*

I might very well expect not only repayment but some show of remorse and a change of heart as well. The wrongdoer in the killing of a pet will be expected to express sorrow and state that they will never do the same again.

In Konstan's chapter on forgiveness in the Bible, he makes a key point. Konstan notes that there are elements of modern forgiveness to be seen as early as the Old Testament. In early Scripture, Konstan observes that God alone undertakes forgiveness—there's no mention of humans forgiving in the same manner. What does God forgive? Israel's errant ways—so that because of God's forgiveness, the people will return to God. The cycle of idolatry, forgiveness, and return to God continues into the New Testament, creating a notion like (in Konstan's mind) but somewhat different from contemporary forgiveness's confession, remorse, and transformation.

We can see how such a cycle might lay the groundwork for the modern understanding of forgiveness that Konstan cites in Griswold—the notion of forgiveness and return to God sounds very much like the contemporary admission of fault, remorse, and the commitment to a change of character. The notion that sets the biblical cycle apart from the modern understanding is the modern understanding of moral autonomy. In a culture of autonomy, there is no return to a loving Creator, but instead a voluntary alignment of ourselves with our notion of goodness. That's quite different both in purpose and in nature. In the former, humanity was created for relationship with God and in the latter humanity identifies with a God that humanity must discover. In the former biblical sense, we return to God following our idolatrous separation from the Creator's love; in the latter humanity voluntarily initiates our reconciliation with the Creator.

Konstan talks about this difference and the critical shortcomings of the modern understanding of forgiveness near the conclusion of his book. He writes, "There is no doubt that forgiveness is widely perceived as an urgent matter these days . . . forgiveness has recommended itself as an especially profound, moral, and effective way of rising above bitterness and resolving conflict. That the demand to grant forgiveness may be coercive, the preconditions for eliciting it may be faked, its efficacy in assuaging rage may be overestimated, and, finally, the very concept may depend on assumptions that are philosophically incoherent—all this is reasonably well-known, and points to the possibility that we are dealing here with a notion that serves a particular ideological function in today's world."[4]

---

4. Konstan, *Before Forgiveness*, location 3796.

Following Konstan's notion that our understanding of forgiveness changes over time, he notes its various failures. It's hard to imagine but the demand that we forgive others (and perhaps even ourselves) can be coercive. Konstan continues that almost all the preconditions for success-ful forgiveness can be faked, including the admission of guilt, any state-ment of remorse, and even the commitment to a change of character. Most damning of all is that the value of this modern forgiveness and its claim to "assuage rage" is grossly overestimated; forgiveness, Konstan suggests, may only serve our ideological devotion to the therapeutic and individual. A friend of mine, a school administrator, agrees. Teachers and administra-tors frequently admonish students to forgive a perpetrator chiefly to allay anger and revenge. Do the students volunteer for this? Not at all, for they must apologize to avoid detention. Altogether then, while we may embrace modern forgiveness we would do well to remember that it's a present-day function of our modern psychology and culture rather than any founda-tional definition of forgiveness. Konstan concludes:

> I have sought to show that the notion of interpersonal forgiveness, as it is basically understood today, is not only not universal but also is of relatively recent coinage, and that the ancient societies to which we often look as models for our ethical concepts—whether classical Greece and Rome, or the Jewish and Christian traditions that emerged within and alongside them—seem to have done per-fectly well without it.[5]

Now that Konstan has established for us the very malleable nature of for-giveness over time, let's turn to see how the idea of forgiveness has changed over time in the Bible.

The History of Forgiveness in the Old Testament

Let's briefly review how history and forgiveness affect one another. As we have seen in both our look at the history of memory (remember Riley and *Inside Out*?) and later in Konstan's work, the understanding of forgiveness has changed over time more than we might at first presume. While the term *forgiveness* may remain the same (though as we will see in the Bible, the words for forgiveness can shift too), viewpoint changes. Context and developing usage have altered our practice of forgiveness. Notably, even

5. Konstan, *Before Forgiveness*, location 3806.

the understanding of apparently permanent human relations such as love and marriage have changed dramatically over human history. So, too, with forgiveness—no single, permanent, foundational definition of forgiveness remains the same in every period of human history.

As much as the meaning of forgiveness changes through human history, so does its meaning change throughout the Bible. In the Old and New Testaments, several different terms have come to be translated as forgiveness. Words translated into English to mean "forgiveness" may also be translated as another term in different biblical circumstances.[6] (In a few moments, you'll read how the NRSV translates the same term as "pardon" in one case, and "forgiveness" in another.) There are roughly only 6,000 words in the biblical Hebrew vocabulary; the context in which a word is used often determines the meaning. We have similar determining uses in English; *coach* can mean a person who directs an athlete or in another context, refer to a vehicle carrying people. Let me show you what I mean in Scripture.

Two Hebrew words that often get translated as "forgiven," "forgive" or "forgiveness" are *nasa* and *salah*. The Hebrew *nasa* commonly refers to the taking away, pardon, or forgiveness of sin. Many times, *nasa* translates as "forgiveness" in the sense that an offense has been done and simply set aside following repayment. For example, and this is often cited by those who speak of interpersonal forgiveness in the Old Testament, *nasa* appears in Genesis 50:17: "Say to Joseph: 'I beg you, *forgive* the crime of your brothers and the wrong they did in harming you. Now therefore please *forgive* the crime of the servants of the God of your father.' Joseph wept when they spoke to him."[7] *Forgive*, in this case, sets aside the offense, even so heinous an offense as Joseph suffered at his brothers' hands.

The story of Joseph, his family, and their entire relationship with Egypt reads as the longest continuous story in the Old Testament. Joseph's brothers treated the young Joseph in a frightful manner, even selling him into slavery. But as Scripture makes clear, God seeks the well-being of the people of Israel, and Joseph became a leader among the Egyptians. In time Joseph's brothers came to Egypt soliciting help in a time of drought and famine in their own land. While in Egypt they are ushered into Joseph's company, unaware that he is their brother, a brother they thought perhaps long dead.

6. Throughout this book, my discussion depends on the New Revised Standard Version unless otherwise noted.

7. Gen 50:17 NRSV.

Joseph surprises the brothers and the brothers beg forgiveness—but not in the full modern sense. The brothers don't pledge to reform in character as a condition of Joseph's forgiveness. They do however want the sin "covered over" and that's what they ask of Joseph—let their fault be as if it never existed. "*Nasa*," take away our sins, the brothers ask, as if they never existed.

Salah often has the sense of lifting or removing in biblical Hebrew. We can catch a sample of the difference between *nasa* and *salah* in Numbers: "*Forgive* (1) the iniquity of this people according to the greatness of your steadfast love, just as you have pardoned this people, from Egypt even until now." Then the LORD said, "I do *forgive*, (2) just as you have asked; nevertheless—as I live, and as all the earth shall be filled with the glory of the LORD—none of the people who have seen my glory and the signs that I did in Egypt and in the wilderness, and yet have tested me these ten times and have not obeyed my voice, shall see the land that I swore to give to their ancestors."[8] The opening "forgive" (1) comes from Moses, petitioning God for pardon. The Hebrew word in that case is *nasa*. However, the second word (2) translated as "forgive," is *salah*. And here lies a critical difference between the two: *nasa* may be requested by a human being but in every case, *salah* can only be provided by God. God alone provides the source of *salah*, and importantly, God alone initiates that forgiveness.

With God as the sole source of this forgiveness, *salah*, we can see how its significance interprets God's forgiveness and how it differs from human forgiveness. This sense of forgiveness we read in *salah* will in time imbue the sense of New Testament forgiveness with enormous spiritual power where New Testament forgiveness comes to reflect Old Testament understandings. Take as an example Isaiah 55:6–9:

> Seek the LORD while he may be found,
>> call upon him while he is near;
> 7   let the wicked forsake their way,
>> and the unrighteous their thoughts;
> let them return to the LORD, that he may have mercy on them,
>> and to our God, for he will abundantly *pardon*.
> 8   For my thoughts are not your thoughts,
>> nor are your ways my ways, says the LORD.
> 9   For as the heavens are higher than the earth,
>> so are my ways higher than your ways

8. Num 14:19–23 NRSV.

and my thoughts than your thoughts.

The "pardon" we read in Isaiah translates *salah*. Now you may be thinking there appears little difference between Isaiah's "pardon," *salah*, and *nasa*, the first forgiveness from Numbers above. However, if we turn to another translation for comparison, Eugene Peterson's *The Message*, we'll catch the full force of "*salah*" in Isaiah:

> Seek GOD while he's here to be found,
> > pray to him while he's close at hand.
> Let the wicked abandon their way of life
> > and the evil their way of thinking.
> Let them come back to GOD, who is merciful,
> > come back to our GOD, who is lavish with *forgiveness*.

Let's reflect on what Isaiah is saying. We are, as the people of Israel, to seek God at all turns, as God always stays with us. Having prayed to God, we should "abandon" our "wicked" way of life and turn to God, a God who is, as Peterson would translate it, "lavish with forgiveness." Let me not burden you with vocabulary study and miss the greater point—God alone offers *salah*, a God who is by nature filled with forgiveness. It follows that we as human beings should turn to God as our present way of life does not serve us well (a good way to describe sin!). Later, in the New Testament church, we find that Isaiah helped the early church shape its theology as a prophetic voice. These echoes of a call from God to humanity to be transformed or converted bring humanity home to the God who created them and loves them. We can certainly hear the voice of Jesus reflected in those words.

One of the heresies that troubled the early church was Marcionism (a heresy sadly perpetuated in our own time). The gist of Marcionism works like this: we read the character of God of the Old Testament as savage and unpredictable. In direct contrast, we read the life of Jesus in the New Testament as peaceful and loving. Therefore, Marcion and his followers concluded we should reject the Old Testament outright. Does that sound familiar? It should, because this heresy affects how we understand the development of biblical forgiveness. Consider the number of times have you heard people complain about the "angry God" of the Old Testament. This opinion depends far more on hearsay than it does on actual reading. Even if contemporary preachers don't condone Marcionism from the pulpit, they often imply it by preaching only on the Gospels or perhaps occasionally on other New Testament lessons.

The heresy of Marcionism does the New Testament and the early church a terrible disservice; the Old Testament (or Hebrew Scriptures) was very much the early church's Bible. Christians must never forget that. The church turned to the Old Testament to find the pattern of Christ's work among them and Isaiah provides some of that pattern. (Isaiah 53, the Suffering Servant, appears in chapters just prior to the Isaiah quote above.) The prophet Isaiah illumines two key topics that we will see again and again in the New Testament: that God initiates forgiveness, and lavishly at that; and secondly, God initiates a call to errant humanity to return to God. Konstan notes that a pattern of forgiveness formed in the Old Testament as first turning away from God and then returning or "conversion." Konstan concludes: "Thus, many of the elements of forgiveness in the rich, modern sense of the term, involving the restoration of a moral relationship between two parties as a consequence of a mutual change of heart, were in place."[9] Konstan hastens to point out that this is not the same as modern forgiveness, and I agree. As we will see in our study of the New Testament and Strand Three, the image of God as unilaterally initiating forgiveness for humanity will become the core of radical Christian forgiveness.

The theme of abandonment or idolatry, followed by God's forgiveness and return, gets reflected in the Old Testament term translated as "repent." The Hebrew word translated as "repent" is *shub*, the root of which means "return." To repent in Hebrew means to return: either turn towards God or in a sense, to change course and take another path. "Repent" means much the same in New Testament language, though in contemporary history "repent" has regularly gathered a pejorative connotation. We can see this in novels and films, such as the work of Flannery O'Connor, where the person calling others to repentance seems terribly, even comically, narrow and judgmental. "Repent," which shares a Latin root with "penance," also reminds us of one step in the modern process of forgiveness—we accept that we have sinned and must now do penance, that is, change our character. While this latter usage has strayed somewhat from the original meaning (much as the sense of forgiveness has changed over time), "repent" has in modern times accrued a judgmental sense for many people.

Let me show you what I mean. Think how differently we might hear the word *shub* or "repent" if we saw God as initiating all forgiveness (*salah*)

9. Konstan, *Before Forgiveness*, location 2377.

and that we, humanity, "*shub*" to return to the Lord. Think of God forgiving unilaterally and then our return to our Creator.

We're jumping ahead for a moment but much the same sense of "repent" takes place in the New Testament world. The powerful opening lines of the Gospel of Mark includes these words: "The time is fulfilled, and the kingdom of God has come near; repent, and believe in the good news." The term Mark uses is *metanoeo*, and commonly translated as "repent." But *metanoeo* shares a prefix with "metamorphosis," and like metamorphosis indicates not just a change of heart or feelings, even reform, but also a shift in direction much as *shub* indicates return. Once again, if we listen closely, we can hear a God who forgives unilaterally (and indeed as John the Baptist indicates, the forgiveness has already begun) and asks only that we return to become citizens of the kingdom of God.

How is this discussion important? We can take away several significant insights. First, God initiates forgiveness to humanity and in doing so invites God's creation into a renewed relationship. Are we required or coerced to accept this forgiveness? By no means. But God in initiating this relationship models for humanity what humanity should imitate, the initiating of forgiveness for one another. We would not, to paraphrase the author of First John,[10] know how to forgive if God had not first forgiven us.

Second, as we saw in the Gospel of Mark, there is a paraphrase of Genesis when the author declares, "The beginning of the good news of Jesus Christ, the Son of God . . . ." John the Baptist calls us to accept the forgiveness God offers to return to the first state of our creation, not only as individuals (though certainly this would be the case) but as members, citizens if you will, of the kingdom of God.[11] John's call hearkens back to the Old Testament (John the Baptist's sole Scripture) and, vitally for contemporary Christians, John's call is in the plural and not the singular. I've heard lay and clergy alike interpret John as if he were calling us as individuals. Not so. If we were to word study all the examples of *salah* in the Old Testament, we would soon discover that God's forgiveness gets offered primarily to a community of persons. Forgiveness by its very nature encompasses two or more people, the offender and the offended at least. Whatever else we can say about forgiveness, we must say that it's a communal activity. God certainly treats it as such.

10. 1 John 4:19 NRSV: "We love because he first loved us."
11. Mark 1:1-4 NRSV.

Last, forgiveness occurs as a time-shaped move. When John the Baptist says, "the time is fulfilled," he means that the movement of history has come to its appointed purpose. That is, to recognize that God has unilaterally initiated forgiveness in Jesus Christ. From the cross and resurrection forward, there's no going back. In our modern sense of forgiveness, especially Strand One therapeutic forgiveness, we see clearly the time-shaped form of forgiveness. To fail to forgive another person is to create a lasting burden for the offended, which might be ourself. If we mean to be relieved of the burden of our resentments, time is of the essence, otherwise festering resentments soon turn into anger and revenge. In Strands Two and Three, time has critical importance too, but as Miroslav Volf suggests, all time is played out against God's appointed end of time, the eschaton, and Volf contends that when we collectively arrive at the eschaton, not only will all be forgiven, all will be *forgotten* as well! Forgiveness, rather than looking only backwards, looks forward with hope to the future.

We turn to one last prime example of forgiveness at work in the Old Testament, the story of Jonah. The story of Jonah and his response to the people of Nineveh played a large part in the figurative mind of the early church, providing us an example of the early church reading the work of Christ through the lens of the Old Testament. While this discussion will hardly exhaust what the Old Testament has to say about forgiveness, I believe we will get the greater sense of what forgiveness means in the Hebrew Scriptures.

When Christians talk about the book of Jonah, most often they speak of Jonah's being swallowed by a whale. No doubt about it, the story makes for great telling, especially to children. From our narrow vantage in history, the message appears clear—do what God asks you to do or you will pay the price! Jonah's being swallowed and spewed out after three days reminded the early church of the resurrection of Jesus after three days in the tomb. But is that the end of the message? Not at all. When the word of God first came to Jonah, God's call to Jonah was to tell Nineveh to turn from their evil ways. Jonah's great reluctance to take on that task in a foreign, Gentile city prompted his running from God and ending up in the belly of the whale. That's the summary of the first two chapters of the book of Jonah. But the third and fourth chapters of Jonah have an equally important message to offer regarding forgiveness. The term "forgiveness" does not appear in Jonah but the book does talk about the God who will "relent and change his mind. He may turn from his fierce anger, so that we do not perish" (Jonah 3:9 NRSV).

In the third chapter, God tells Jonah, "Get up, go to Nineveh, that great city, and proclaim to it the message that I tell you."[12] Jonah went to the city of Nineveh (again, a Gentile city, and emphatically not Israel) and proclaims God's message. If Nineveh doesn't turn from their evil ways, in forty days they will be "overthrown." To Jonah's incredulous surprise, the people of Nineveh listened to him, even their king! It's the king of Nineveh who I quoted earlier saying, "Who knows? God may relent and change his mind." The book of Jonah reports this nearly miraculous occurrence, that the Gentile people abruptly changed. Jonah then says, "When God saw what they did, how they turned from their evil ways, God changed his mind about the calamity that he had said he would bring upon them; and he did not do it."[13]

End of story, neatly tied up, or so it would seem at first. But no, this stiff-necked, resentful Jonah will not have it! The book reports, "But this was very displeasing to Jonah, and he became angry. He prayed to the Lord and said, 'O Lord! Is not this what I said while I was still in my own country? That is why I fled to Tarshish at the beginning; for I knew that you are a gracious God and merciful, slow to anger, and abounding in steadfast love, and ready to relent from punishing. And now, O Lord, please take my life from me, for it is better for me to die than to live."[14] Here's the rub as far as Jonah's concerned—even though Jonah knows as he says that God is slow to anger and abounding in mercy, he still wants these Gentiles punished. What is God thinking having put Jonah through so much?

God responds to Jonah by asking if it's right for Jonah to be so angry. Jonah, resentful and perhaps pouting, retreats to the east of the city, disappointed that Nineveh, this vexing city, was not blasted into oblivion! As the story continues, Jonah shows his anger again when God destroys a bush that offered Jonah shade in the wilderness. Jonah angrily states, "It is better for me to die than to live."[15] Sounds like a petulant two-year-old, doesn't he? But the book continues. God said to Jonah, "Is it right for you to be angry about the bush?" And he said, "Yes, angry enough to die." Then the Lord said, "You are concerned about the bush, for which you did not labor and which you did not grow; it came into being in a night and perished in

12. Jonah 3:2 NRSV.
13. Jonah 3:10 NRSV.
14. Jonah 4:1–4 NRSV.
15. Jonah 4:8 NRSV.

a night. And should I not be concerned about Nineveh, that great city, in which there are more than a hundred and twenty thousand persons who do not know their right hand from their left, and also many animals?"[16]

The book of Jonah concludes with this reprimand from God to Jonah, a reprimand the we will hear echoed in New Testament encounters. Later, Jesus will cite Jonah and Nineveh's example in the Gospels: "The people of Nineveh will rise up at the judgment with this generation and condemn it, because they repented at the proclamation of Jonah, and see, something greater than Jonah is here!" (Matthew 12:41 and Luke 11:32, NRSV). Once again, God initiates forgiveness to God's creation (and more than just the people of Israel but also including the Gentiles). While Jonah was disappointed, the people of Nineveh immediately acknowledged their evil. God relented, displaying the "steadfast love," grace, and mercy of which Jonah had already spoken. Nineveh's faults, whatever they may have been, are forgiven. But not by Jonah, and herein lies one aspect of the critical message to the early church—with God disposed to relent and forgive, we, the followers of Christ, should be too. Humanity may not judge the people worthy, especially Gentiles, but that's not the way of God. God appears always disposed to forgive because of God's evident love, grace, and mercy. Even Gentiles. Even and especially in the Old Testament.

I could say much more about God's forgiveness as seen in the Old Testament. But I think we could agree, that despite the Marcion-like protests about the angry God of the Hebrew Scriptures, God's character is disposed to forgive. God forgives generously, gracefully, and lovingly. There's still more evidence that the popular image of the Old Testament God flies in the face of how God's portrayed in some minds. Far from being cruel and exacting, God seeks to forgive. Many people in the time of Jesus will misread or forget what the prophets have said. Ezekiel 18:20 says, "A child shall not suffer for the iniquity of a parent, nor a parent suffer for the iniquity of a child; the righteousness of the righteous shall be his own, and the wickedness of the wicked shall be his own." In other words, the punishment for sinning is not inherited from generation to generation in order that the innocent might be punished for the sins of the fathers and mothers. God forgives. Turning to the Gospel of John, we find that even the disciples believe that sins are inherited. When Jesus heals the man born blind, the disciples ask, "Rabbi, who sinned, this man or his parents, that he was born blind?" Jesus answered, "Neither this man nor his parents sinned; he was

16. Jonah 4:9–11 NRSV.

born blind so that God's works might be revealed in him."[17] The prophet Ezekiel anticipates the Lord's disposition to forgive many generations before the resurrection of Christ. In God's creation infirmity is not a punishment, forgiveness is a given. The sense of forgiveness in the Old Testament is richly nuanced but God is always disposed to forgive. Return, "*shub*," to the Creator and be included in the kingdom of God.

The History of Forgiveness in the New Testament

Some people mistakenly think of the New Testament as the sole source for biblical forgiveness. The God of the Old Testament presumably rules only with fiery judgement. I hope that I have persuaded you otherwise and that you see that the Old Testament contains a deep and abiding sense of forgiveness. Indeed, the Scriptures of the Old Testament, sometimes called "the Hebrew Scriptures," became a fount of imagery and spiritual nourishment for the New Testament. In the coming pages, we will look chiefly at the Gospel of Matthew, though we must also consider the parable of the Prodigal Son in the Gospel of Luke. Why not all the Gospels? Why not more Paul? Because they are just too rich and broad a resource to be covered in brief. Matthew, and a few other New Testament letters, will give us a good appreciation of how forgiveness came to be seen in the New Testament.

Jesus, turning to the Old Testament, cites the story of Jonah as an example of forgiveness, or at least the need for forgiveness at work. In Matthew, Jesus points twice to the example of Jonah and the people of Nineveh repenting. Jesus said to the people, "An evil and adulterous generation asks for a sign, but no sign will be given to it except the sign of the prophet Jonah. For just as Jonah was three days and three nights in the belly of the sea monster, so for three days and three nights the Son of Man will be in the heart of the earth. The people of Nineveh will rise up at the judgment with this generation and condemn it, because they repented at the proclamation of Jonah, and see, something greater than Jonah is here." (Matt 12:39–41 and similarly in Matthew 16:7; we have a parallel in Luke 11:29–32.) Jesus in Matthew treats the story of Jonah as an allegorical instruction. Jonah was three days in the whale and so too will the Son of Man be buried in the earth. What will happen? The people of Nineveh who repented despite Jonah's disposition not to spare them, will in turn become a source of judgment for this "generation," that is, the people of the time of Jesus. But more

17. John 9:2 NRSV.

yet may be said for the people of Nineveh were Gentiles and that they re-ceived God's forgiveness necessarily extends God's care beyond Israel, "the people of this generation." Further, Jesus allegorically points to himself as a prophet after the likes of Jonah, sent to a world reluctant to hear the truth. Will this generation listen? Only their response to his crucifixion and res-urrection will tell.

I think sometimes we need to be reminded of what should be self-evident—the only Scripture the New Testament church possessed was the Hebrew Scriptures, the Old Testament. Just as in today's world, including among the unchurched, the story of Jonah was widely known to the people of Israel. Nearly everyone would have known the allusion of Jesus to the three days in the belly of the whale. More broadly yet, the story of Jonah invites a rich interpretation. God called Jonah to prophecy and because Jonah attempted to hide, God sent Jonah to the belly of the whale. While the reasons were different for Jonah and Jesus, the process shared much in common. God was the agent of salvation for Jonah and Nineveh and God was the agent of salvation for Jesus and Israel, and for the world. The chief difference between the people listening to Jesus and those in our time is the awareness of what happened after Jonah was spewed out on the beach. Modern Sunday school storybooks often leave out Jonah's reluctance to for-give, pinning attention on the time in the whale's belly. I remember sharing the story of Jonah, the whale, and his unforgiving relationship with the people of Nineveh with a Sunday school class in my parish. I was struck by the parents and teachers who came up to me after the class, remarking how they had never known about Jonah's angry reluctance to forgive. "So, this was a story about forgiveness?" The parents and teachers had not known.

While some modern readers are troubled by allegorical readings of the Old Testament, clearly the New Testament was not. The early church and much of the Gospels read the allegorical pattern for the life of Jesus in Isaiah. Isaiah speaks of how the Suffering Servant, as the central figure of Chapter 53 was described, was "despised and rejected." This Servant, Isaiah reports, "has borne our infirmities and carried our diseases" and in time "he was wounded for our transgressions, crushed for our iniquities." Isaiah then makes this most astonishing claim in ancient literature, that "he was wounded for our transgressions, crushed for our iniquities; upon him was the punishment that made us whole, and by his bruises we are healed. All we like sheep have gone astray; we have all turned to our own way, and the LORD has laid on him the iniquity of us all." To what end did the Servant suffer all this abuse? To the end that he will "make his life an offering for sin" and that the Servant "bore the sins of many, and made intercession for the transgressors" (Isa 53:3–12).

Modern people sometimes fail to grasp how very singular this image of the Suffering Servant was for the ancient world. For most ancient societies, justice was established through might, and right was solely an entitlement of those who held the reins of power. The idea that a human could transform the world by suffering on behalf of others, a person who could bring justice by passively accepting the violence of others, would have been beyond most people's ken. We don't have the space to unpack all the implications of the Suffering Servant but you can see plainly how the Servant proved to be a prophetic figure to the early church of Jesus' own suffering. Jesus continued to win people not by oppression or violence but by patiently suffering the death inflicted by the powers of this world. And Jesus won the victory not by violently winning the war but by the greater victory of surmounting death. Could you imagine a more radical approach to forgiveness than that of the Suffering Servant? Just as in the Latin root, that is, *radical*—this Servant became the root of an entirely new fruit.

Some believe that the New Testament took the story of the Suffering Servant wholesale from the Old and applied it to the life of Jesus. To their minds the entire story of Jesus became a kind of fiction based on Isaiah. This undermines the power of the prophetic unity between the Old and New Testaments. Even so, the prophecy of Isaiah did come to pass, the man Jesus, the Son of Man, was in fact crucified, a fact no one denies. Moreover, with the insight of the prophet Isaiah and other prophets, the early church came to understand the history of the longing of God to forgive God's creation. Like an enormous spring bubbling out of the earth, the story of forgiveness that we discovered in the Old Testament will find its way in the New, nourishing and causing the gift of forgiveness to further flourish in these new scriptures and in the infant church.

The word most often translated as 'forgiveness' in the New Testament comes from the Greek word *aphimei*. In classic Greek, the term had overtones of "sending off, hurl, pardon or release."[18] Surveying the New Testament, you would discover that very rarely was the term used in relationship to the relief of debt. By the time the term was taken up in the New Testament, the Greek had come to mean something like "let go, to leave, to leave behind, to let alone, to allow." Those latter meanings are important

18. Bromiley, ed., *Theological Dictionary of the New Testament*, 88.

because they point far beyond the metaphor that forgiveness is a simple settling of a debt. To get a sense of how differently the term *aphimei* works in a case where *aphimei* is *not* translated as forgiveness, let's look at Matthew 27:50. There Matthew reports, "Then Jesus cried again with a loud voice and breathed his last." *Aphimei* in this case translates as Jesus "gave up his breath." No debt was implied, no pardon included. If we translate *aphimei* into the modern vernacular, we'd likely translate the word as "let it go." You will note that we cannot read backward from the modern concept of forgiveness into the word *aphimei*. To "let go" in forgiveness excludes the modern sense of forgiveness that includes mutual recognition of the offense, including reform and a change of heart. Indeed, the New Testament sense of forgiveness was in a sense much broader, deeper, and more radical than either the modern or classical sense of forgiveness.

In the New Testament, forgiveness, *aphimei*, was almost always attributed to God, or God in Jesus Christ. Not unlike the Old Testament, in the New Testament humanity doesn't initiate forgiveness. Even though humanity will be called to forgive in imitation of God, God alone initiates forgiveness. God's forgiveness provides the source of forgiveness, and God gives freely.

There are objections to the notion that God's forgiveness is complete unto itself. Some scholars object, particularly considering the modern understanding of forgiveness, that repentance and reconciliation were required by Jesus. In short you can't be forgiven if you don't first repent and then seek to reconcile. There's a quid pro quo in their mind that we cannot receive forgiveness if we don't forgive others. We must tread carefully here; we need to be able to distinguish between some sense of economic exchange (the notion that forgiveness is transactional—that you will receive by the measure you give) and a more enduring, radical Christian forgiveness.

One of the most often cited examples of God requiring forgiveness from humanity comes from the Lord's Prayer. As it's translated in the NRSV, the prayer begins in Matthew 6:9 with "Our father in heaven," and continues with "Give us this day our daily bread. And forgive us our debts as we also have forgiven our debtors." Often, and this is very important to our understanding of forgiveness, people regard this petition that humanity, being desirous of forgiveness, must first forgive others to secure our own forgiveness. There it is, quid pro quo. But the interpretation that we "get as we give" leaves out some significant shading of meaning found in the Greek. The first verb "forgive" in the Lord's Prayer has the grammatical sense of something already done, something perfected and accomplished. That form of *aphimei* appears in the "imperative" sense, meaning that either that sense of "forgive" stipulates a command or more accurately in this case, an action that's necessary or at least very important. Eugene Peterson, in *The Message*, translates this grammatically cumbersome passage this way: "Keep us forgiven with you and forgiving others." However trying the reading may be, Peterson has succeeded in capturing the sense of the Greek (at least to the extent you can directly do so in English). In other words, as the prayer begins those who are praying acknowledge that *they have already been forgiven*. Already forgiven! Now in the second "forgive," the Greek has that same grammatical sense of an action already perfected but stated as a fact. If I were to supply my own translation, the petition would read something like this: "You have already forgiven us, God, and let us never forget that others have already been forgiven too, a forgiveness that we must imitate." No quid pro quo here but instead a solemn acknowledgement that all of us have already been forgiven, a forgiveness shared that truly binds us together in our humanity.

I've spent significant time unpacking Greek grammar (though I'm not a Greek scholar) but to a very important end. As you can read, this interpretation of the Lord's Prayer strays far from a simple transaction, we only get as we give. Instead, I want to emphasize that in this translation, those who are praying the Lord's Prayer acknowledge that they have already been forgiven. Simply praying the Prayer shows your acceptance that you have become a forgiven person. Forgiveness is not a prize won at the expense of our forgiving others, as a paid exchange for forgiving others. The other people have already been forgiven too; our job is to echo or imitate God's behavior in our bonding relationships with the others. I can't make this point too strongly—*God has already forgiven us in the cross of Christ*. Our job now is to learn how, as Stanley Hauerwas has said, "to learn to live as a forgiven people."[19] Humanity, and more particularly, ourselves, may not have requested forgiveness and certainly not sought it in our actions, and yet God in Jesus Christ has already forgiven us, radically forgiven us, and perhaps to our surprise, everyone else as well!

Does this reading of the Lord's Prayer fly in the face of everything you've learned about forgiveness? That your forgiveness is conditional on your being a forgiving person? I suspect it does because it certainly was a key aspect of my Christian formation, even into adulthood. But think back

19. Quoted in Jones, *Embodying Forgiveness*, 148.

to Konstan's history of forgiveness: Konstan outlines an understanding of forgiveness that he believes has only existed for some 150 years—if we are the offended, we must agree with the offender about the nature of the crime, secure the offender's apology, and finally, the offender's commitment to lasting reform. A neat and perfectly useful interpretation in a society that prizes an economic satisfaction among individuals.

Howsoever many holes we can discover in this contemporary view of forgiveness, this modern form of forgiveness has become the established norm for our practice. Those of us who have been led to believe that terms like *love, courage,* and *forgiveness* must have some timeless, foundational definition, are going to be sadly disappointed. And we'll be frustrated too when we try to extend our modern understanding of forgiveness back through time on to New Testament forgiveness. If Konstan is correct, the restraints we place on exercising forgiveness in our modern life were foreign to the New Testament forgiveness of Jesus.

Matthew 18 has sometimes been called "the handbook of the ancient church." Many practices of communal church life were addressed in this chapter but among the most important is forgiveness. In fact, large parts of the chapter address forgiveness from several different perspectives. In Matthew 18:15–31 we have a remarkable progression of stages for invoking forgiveness within the infant church community. The first verse begins with, "If another member of the church sins against you, go and point out the fault when the two of you are alone. If the member listens to you, you have regained that one." Matthew continues, "But if you are not listened to, take one or two others along with you, so that every word may be confirmed by the evidence of two or three witnesses. If the member refuses to listen to them, tell it to the church; and if the offender refuses to listen even to the church, let such a one be to you as a Gentile and a tax collector."

There are several notable developments in this progression. First, this view of forgiveness encourages progress in its development. Rather than treat forgiveness as an absolute on-and-off, black-and-white form of forgiveness between individuals, the Gospel understands forgiveness as open-ended. In a fashion, the Gospel takes the view that the effort to secure forgiveness is worth many more than one overture between people. Jesus in Matthew 18 makes the case that the offender has so much value that we should return again and again to forgiving the offender.

Second, the whole notion of forgiveness is not constrained to an undertaking between individuals; if needed, the entire community of the church can be involved. By stepping carefully along in the effort to solicit forgiveness, Matthew 18 avoids shame being heaped on the offender but at the same time, the progression of efforts recognizes implicitly that forgiveness is the community standard.

Last, the view that if the offender refused to be forgiven, that the offender should be treated as "a Gentile and a tax collector" invites some reflection on the context of Matthew. Matthew has been traditionally understood to have been written by just such a person, a Gentile and tax collector. In that case, this treatment of the offender invites an open-ended rather than closed-ended approach; if Matthew can become a forgiven member of the community, who can be excluded?

This interpretation gets abetted by the following verse: "Truly I tell you, whatever you bind on earth will be bound in heaven, and whatever you loose on earth will be loosed in heaven." This verse has another parallel earlier in Matthew: "I will give you the keys of the kingdom of heaven, and whatever you bind on earth will be bound in heaven, and whatever you loose on earth will be loosed in heaven." A similar verse appears in the John 20:23 in the resurrection appearance of Jesus to the disciples, where Jesus commissions the disciples to forgive sins: "When he had said this, he breathed on them and said to them, 'Receive the Holy Spirit. If you forgive the sins of any, they are forgiven them; if you retain the sins of any, they are retained.'" Some traditions, especially liturgical traditions, have treated these last lines as indicating the need for the priestly absolution of the church. But there's another way to read these verses. We might be better to read the verses to say something like this: "Whatever you forgive on earth will be forgiven in heaven; whatever you hang on to on earth, will remain with you as a continuing burden." Certainly, the parallel in the Gospel of John reads that way. The point is to assume your treatment of others with the utmost gravity, for as Peterson translates this passage in *The Message*, "Take this most seriously: A yes on earth is yes in heaven; a no on earth is no in heaven. What you say to one another is eternal. I mean this." When it comes to forgiving sins, if we as the church fail to say "yes" to people, they and we may be burdened with our "no" forever.

Later in Matthew 18, Peter, ever the overachiever among the disciples, asks Jesus, "Lord, if another member of the church sins against me, how often should I forgive? As many as seven times?" Of course, we can never know for sure what was going through Peter's mind but based on other encounters with Peter in the Gospel, we may presume that he was demonstrating that he had a firm grasp on this teaching. Jesus responds to Peter by saying, "Not seven times, but, I tell you, seventy-seven times." Seventy-seven times! Peter has widely missed the mark.

Many years ago, when I taught in public school, it seemed as if every class had a student who threw their hand up with an answer before everyone else in class— "I know, I know!" Perhaps that was Peter. I believe that what Peter originally intended was to show how generous his picture of forgiveness was—forgive one another not just once or twice but as many as seven times. That must have seemed magnanimous to him. But Jesus goes far beyond Peter's magnanimity—Jesus teaches that we should forgive at least seventy-seven times! (Cf. Luke 17:1–4 for a slightly different take.) Seventy-seven times! Not only does that expectation demonstrate a superabundance of forgiveness but it's telling us, and subsequently, the church, how we should practice forgiveness. Perhaps it would be helpful to think about our relations with a spouse as an example of forgiving seventy-seven times. I can hardly imagine myself saying to my spouse, "That's sixty-nine times I've forgiven you; you only get eight more!" Ridiculous, isn't it? If I were so obsessively keeping count of my acts of forgiveness, I think we would not judge my forgiveness as forgiveness but instead as an obsessive-compulsive disorder or some kind of psychosis. No, when Jesus teaches we should forgive seventy-seven times he clearly wants to disrupt the notion that forgiveness should be treated as if it has limits. Forgiveness cannot be treated as a set of rules to be followed or an accountant's process but instead as open-ended and as grace-filled as Jesus himself.

Does that mean that forgiveness does not include reproof? At least within the church, it may. Jesus said, "Be on your guard! If another disciple sins, you must rebuke the offender, and if there is repentance, you must forgive."[20] Some scholars believe that this verse from the Gospel of Luke was a later addition, a redaction, from scribes of the early church. But if not, it's an important way to view forgiveness within the body of the church. Forgiveness reigns over reproof. But to support the dissenting scholars point, the following verse reads: "if the same person sins against you seven times a day, and turns back to you seven times and says, 'I repent,' you must forgive." I cannot imagine a more open-ended attitude towards forgiveness. We must develop a patient disposition to forgiveness in all circumstances if we wish to follow Christ.

20. Luke 17:3.

As a side note, this sense of the disciples, especially Peter, developing a "disposition" plays a critical part in the development of discipleship. Earlier in Matthew 16:16, Peter declares to Jesus, "You are the Messiah, the Son of the living God." Exactly right. Jesus then goes on to say that he must be humiliated, die, and be resurrected, a prophecy to which Peter objects. Surely Jesus need not go through this! Jesus responds by telling Peter that he's Satan, a stumbling block, for Peter "sets his mind" on human things, not on divine things. In this case, I think I need to unpack the Greek a bit. The phrase translated as "stumbling block" in English is *skandalon* in the Greek. You can see the shared root with "scandal," right? But then Jesus goes on to say that the *phronesis* of Peter reflects human concerns, not God's way of thinking. The term *phronesis*, often referring in classical Greek to talk about how we virtuously develop character, means a manner of thinking, a habit, a focus if you will, a disposition. In other words, given the choice between a human disposition and a divine one, Peter has chosen the former. Peter has developed a character of Satan-like practices, more human than divine. Peter needs to change to virtues reflecting God's disposition.

Phronesis gets to be very important in our habituated responses to events—if we were thinking like God, we will habitually respond in one fashion, if like humans, likely in another. Why is this important? Because if Jesus characterizes our most common disposition this way, we know that we can be trained to think, or be disposed differently towards others in another fashion than the one we already practice. In other words, we can develop better habits including, in this case, a habit of forgiving as God forgives. Does Jesus think Peter should be divine? Likely not, but he does believe that Peter can develop a disciplined habit of forgiving others without thought for himself.

The last example from Matthew comes right after the admonition to Peter to forgive seventy-seven times. In this story, which demonstrates how things are to be done in the kingdom of Heaven, Jesus tells a story of enormous, unsurpassable forgiveness; a forgiveness very much beyond human reckoning, even considering a required forgiveness of seventy-seven times. The king in this story has a servant brought to him who owes him "ten thousand talents." The king forgives the servant this debt. In the mind of the naive, this is a debt to be sure but still just a debt. If, however, scale and amount matter, ten thousand talents represents a stupendous number in New Testament times—roughly a billion dollars in our era. Do you see the point Jesus makes? No servant could ever hope to pay off a debt of this magnitude nor would any king in the ancient world (and certainly in our world, considering the failure to relieve Third World debt) ever abolish a debt of this size. We don't have far to leap to see how Jesus would regard the extraordinary forgiveness of the king as a figure for the king of the kingdom of Heaven. In sum, in the face of an impossible debt, only God's forgiveness alone can relieve it.

That's not the end of the story. When the same servant who was forgiven a billion dollars encounters someone who owes him a debt, representing about a hundred days' wages, the servant who had experienced the king's extraordinary generosity demands that the other servant pay up, now. The other servant cannot and so the one who had experienced a vast forgiveness throws into prison the one who seeks a much smaller forgiveness of debt. Friends of the imprisoned servant hear about this injustice and tell the king. The king is furious and so imprisons the servant who had been forgiven the greater debt, for his lack of compassion and generosity. The king had the unforgiving servant tortured until he could pay his entire debt.

Very often people point to this story as an example of God requiring that we forgive others before we ourselves can be forgiven. There's no question that the unforgiving servant stands under judgment—he has sinned as excessively as he was forgiven. Certainly, we can read this story that way and many people have. But we can also read it from another perspective, from the gesture of magnanimous forgiveness and see the outcome differently. The sense that God will forgive so extravagantly sets the emphasis that God can and will forgive without measure. If we as humanity will stand under judgement for anything, it's because we don't do the same—we do not forgive after the fashion that we have already been forgiven.

The notion that we must "forgive from our heart" appears only this one time in all the Gospels. The singular nature of this instruction makes it all the more important. Remembering Peter and *phronesis*, we can catch the sense of a habitual action. We forgive not with the heart as a single source of forgiveness but as the ever-beating heart of life itself. We learn the disposition to forgive and make forgiveness a habitual practice. Failure to do so lands us under judgment.

The king's judgment of the unforgiving servant compares in extravagance to the forgiveness of a billion dollars. Pointedly, no one could ever hope to repay a billion dollars while being tortured—clearly this is hyperbole. Like plucking out our eye or cutting off our offending hand, this story serves as an incredibly rich allegory of how God forgives magnanimously and that we too should follow God's example. If we don't, we will be burdened with sins, possibly forever, and stand always under God's judgment for not becoming habitual forgivers. The magnanimity of God's forgiveness surprises us with its graceful compassion; we too should surprise others with our forgiveness.

I have a gift for you, a surprising reading of everyone's favorite parable, the Prodigal Son. Amy Jill Levine, a Jewish scholar and student of the New Testament, has studied the parables of Jesus as if they were Jewish short stories in her book *Short Stories of Jesus*.[21] The parable of the Prodigal Son doesn't appear in Matthew, the Gospel we have been studying, but the parable of the Prodigal Son's enormous popularity recommends that we reflect on it. Most interpretations of the Prodigal Son go something like this: there was a man with two sons, one of whom, the younger, was selfish, impetuous, and a greedy sinner. The younger son, hell-bent on having a good time, demands from his aging father his half of the family fortune, a demand both pretentious and socially outrageous. The prodigal leaves for the unclean lands of the Gentiles, where he blows the whole fortune on dissolute living. Shorn of his wealth, he returns home to his father, who welcomes him with open arms, even though presumably he is now unclean. The older brother gets jealously angry and we worry about his reluctance to forgive his brother as his father has forgiven him. Sound familiar? I believe that account represents the most common reading of the parable of the Prodigal Son. I've certainly read reputable scholars who interpret the story in that fashion. But Levine offers a different view, one that may sound peculiar to us and yet entirely in sync with what we've discovered so far about New Testament forgiveness.

Levine begins her book with this caution on reading the parables: "We might be better off thinking less about what [the parables] 'mean' and more about what they can 'do': remind, provoke, refine, confront, disturb . . . ."[22] Levine correctly observes that Christians often read the parables as object lessons. The reading of the prodigal as a moral fable of dissolute failure does just that, cautioning people with an object lesson while inviting them to repent. (I have joked in sermons that parishioners rather like identifying with the younger son, spendthrift, heedless, and carefree, though most of us behave like the elder!) But Levine's take on the story goes another

21. Levine, *Short Stories of Jesus*.
22. Levine, *Short Stories of Jesus*, 4,

direction, not as a caution against prodigality, but rather as an encouragement to attentive, magnanimous forgiveness.

Levine begins her comments by reminding us what first-century Jews would have heard when Jesus told this parable. The listeners would have been reminded immediately of other Old Testament stories about pairs of brothers like Cain and Abel or Jacob and Esau. Moreover, because of the stories the listeners knew so well, they would have been inclined to identify the younger son with successful sons like Joseph, David, or Solomon. Levine also reminds us that the younger son asking for his inheritance was not uncommon or against the grain in the first century any more than it is in our time. In my pastoral experience, it happens more often than you might think. The challenge in reading the story in the context of first-century Judaism stems from allegorizing the brothers' father as God—in no way would those listeners have imagined the father as God, even though we're inclined to do so in our time. Levine makes a critical point: "There is no compelling reason in the parable itself to see the father as God, but even if Jesus' Jewish audience had made this connection, they would have found nothing surprising. The covenant is still in place; God still loves the wayward, from David to Ephraim to Israel."[23] "God still loves the wayward," whomever they may be! How do we know this? Because of God's one-sided covenant with humankind. That is, God reached out in love to be joined with God's creation, especially humanity, without at the same time requiring humanity's reciprocal affection. Though not as well known to some people in the pews, one of the most wondrous overtures of God towards humanity was God's unilateral establishment of a covenant with God's people. Unlike a contract that requires two parties to ratify the agreement, this covenant was entirely initiated by God, loving and overflowing with God's generous concern for us. Scripture reports that the rainbow became a sign of that covenant between God and humanity.

Levine points out that the story of the prodigal was joined with two parables of loss in the Gospel of Luke, parables of finding and celebration, the parable of the Lost Sheep and of the Lost Coin. The outcome of all three parables was shared happiness and feasting at the recovery of the lost! Levine's most important point in the story of the prodigal is that the "lost" is not the younger son as Christians have been led to believe—he returns home like a bad penny, taking advantage of all! —but the truly "lost" was the older brother. To be sure, the father doesn't recognize this at first but

23. Levine, *Short Stories of Jesus*, 57.

as Levine writes, "Once the recognition comes, he does what the shepherd with the lost sheep and the woman with the lost coin do: realizing his loss, his lost son, the son whom he loves, he seeks to make his family whole. He pleads with him."[24] Levine contends that the younger son has done nothing more than what he has always done, "take advantage of the father's love. And yet his father loves him, and he is a member of the family. Therefore, he cannot be ignored, and to dismiss him would be to dismiss the father as well."[25] Despite the continuing need to welcome the younger son, according to Levine, the parable focus falls chiefly on the elder—how can he be returned to the fold? How can he be persuaded to rejoin the family, much as God's covenant would desire of Israel? Levine's closing point is worth quoting at length:

> If we hold in abeyance, at least for the moment, the rush to read repenting and forgiving into the parable, then it does something more profound than repeat well-known messages. It provokes us with simple exhortations. Recognize that the one you have lost may be right in your own household. Do whatever it takes to find the lost and then celebrate with others, so that you can share the joy and so that the other will help prevent the recovered from ever being lost again. Don't wait until you receive an apology; you may never get one. Don't wait until you can muster the ability to forgive; you may never find it. . . . If the repenting and forgiving come later, so much the better. And if not, you still will have done what is necessary. You will have begun a process that might lead to reconciliation. You will have opened a second chance for wholeness. Take advantage of resurrection—it is unlikely to happen twice.[26]

The parable of the Prodigal Son does "do" something very important, and that is that it provokes us to act much as God acts with Israel, forgiving and welcoming even if the offender is unrepentant. God's covenant remains the covenant under every condition despite or even because humanity may ignore it.

What then does all this mean about forgiveness in the New Testament? Arguably, I believe that God's forgiveness can be read as largely prevenient, that is, that God forgives through Jesus Christ long before humanity asks. Does that mean that humanity need not repent or that humanity does not stand under judgment? By no means, but our understanding of forgiveness

24. Levine, *Short Stories of Jesus*, 63.
25. Levine, *Short Stories of Jesus*, 69.
26. Levine, *Short Stories of Jesus*, 69.

has shifted from the modern understanding of forgiveness in a very important way, that there are steps that must be followed, that forgiveness is in the end conditional. Long before we admit our wrongs, our sins, long before or even without repentance, even prior to any pledge on our part to change our character or convert, God forgives through the cross of Christ. *The cross of Christ was God's judgement and the predetermined outcome of that judgment was forgiveness.*

I know that some people will find that last claim troubling and perhaps controversial. And I don't believe my claim stands as indisputable. And yet like the parable of the Workers hired late in the day, receiving the same wage as those hired at the first of day,[27] the economy of God's grace appears upside-down to humanity. I believe that the New Testament's vision of forgiveness may be just as upside-down compared to our modern, secular picture of forgiveness. Just for that reason, I would contend that the biblical understanding of forgiveness is even more welcome. How many times should we forgive? At least seventy-seven times, far more times than any of us may count.

27. Matt 20:1–16.

5

Exploring the First Strand

I SAW A THOUGHT-PROVOKING cartoon in *The New Yorker* some time ago. A pensive dog had his face pressed to the rear window of a car. The cartoon caption read: "He'd barked and barked as she made her way into the pharmacy, yet all the resentment and anger was now washed away as he worked his way through the nine steps of forgiveness." I can't think of a better illustration to introduce the First Strand of Forgiveness, a strand devoted almost entirely to the secular, popular understanding of forgiveness. To my mind, the artist captured with gentle humor both the therapeutic value and, at the same time, the irony of modern secular forgiveness. While I clearly come down on the side of Christian forgiveness, with an emphasis on radical Christian forgiveness, I recognize the value and contribution of secular forgiveness. Let me be plain—absent a Christian community of convictions and practices, I believe we do in fact need individual resources to forgive in our modern society. We need skills to cope with and relinquish both resentment and anger. We need a pathway to reconciliation even if not led in that pathway by faith.

Forgiveness plays a critical part in the modern psyche. Psychologists have long recognized how corrosive resentments can be; in fact, artists have often made angry resentment a cornerstone of modern tragic writing and films. As an important example, the Twelve Steps of Alcoholics Anonymous work hard to eradicate resentments, strongly acknowledging what impediment resentments become for recovery from addiction. While psychologists and philosophers remain divided about the place of anger in our lives,[1] nearly all of them acknowledge that long-term anger can bring

1. See Nussbaum, *Anger and Forgiveness.*

on depression, disease, and even death. So, yes, we need to learn to forgive, including in a secular culture. That said, we need to probe the practices involved and their underpinnings to see their place in our lives.

For Christians, the key practice of forgiving is born of our imitation of God's relationship to humanity, especially through the life of Christ. Christians seek to imitate Christ. But what if we are not devoted to following the example of Christ? What if we are simply oblivious or misinformed about the example of Christ or more commonly, just don't believe? What if we indeed live in a culture whose values are entirely, definitively secular? The secular view of life and particularly of forgiveness, can and does color the church's view of forgiveness. But for now, let's look at Strand One, both to unpack its value and to critique its contribution.

In the brief space we have, it's simply impossible to give an exhaustive analysis of secular forgiveness. Remember? There are some 13,000 books and publications alone that in some fashion or another deal with forgiveness. Undeniably, amongst those books are many different perspectives on forgiveness; there's no means by which we can include them all. But I believe if we approach secular forgiveness chiefly in terms of "therapeutic forgiveness," we'll be able to capture much of the essence of modern secular forgiveness, or what I call Strand One.

Why the term *therapeutic?* Because when we speak of therapy, we have in mind practices that lead to the restoration of health, in body and in mind, to restore an essentially healthy human being. This sense of the therapeutic arguably governs much of modern life in the past 150 years but most especially the twentieth and twenty-first centuries. At its core, I believe the therapeutic view of humanity depends on the deep-seated cultural conviction that human beings are autonomous individuals. These individuals are essentially good and humanity can expect an evolving progress for humanity, constantly improving who and what we are. In these past two centuries, many people have come to believe that the culture that forms us and from which we spring has only our best interests as its purpose. As individuals, and especially as consumers, our self-definition is our prerogative by natural right. In the process of developing our self-definition (and our growing value to ourselves), we have the freedom to become anyone or anything we wish. We have come to believe we are no longer governed by the antiquated and dogmatic claimed certainties of the past, certainties about religion and culture that have often been found bankrupt in our view. From the depths of our humanity we wonder indeed who are we to judge others, others who have in their individualistic way undertaken a journey of self-discovery. Who are we to say what's more right and more wrong in a pluralistic age where values have been relativized and often found empty of meaning?

Sound familiar? I think it should. Is there a problem? In 1965, Philip Reiff published a book entitled *The Uses of Faith after Freud; The Triumph of the Therapeutic*. Fifty years later, the subtitle reveals much of Reiff's critical theme—where we as a culture, at least in the West, once valued a common faith, we have become unmoored from that connection. Having turned faith into an act of voluntary consumption, we have removed to a more rational distance its fundamental character-shaping of our lives. If we are believers, it's because we seek to be. If we are believers, it's because we choose to be and not because we inherited a culture of faith. Absent that historical belief, we fall back on the fundamental character of humanity as developed by figures such as Sigmund Freud and Carl Jung. We are now by definition fundamentally secular self-created beings who may, for various self-affirming reasons, voluntarily associate ourselves with faith but not without the proper cautions. Reiff has been by no means the sole critic of this "therapeutic" view of humanity; theologians, philosophers and sociologists such as Christopher Lasch, David Noble, Charles Taylor, Alistair McIntyre, Kathryn Tanner, John Milbank, and Stanley Hauerwas have continued to develop this criticism. To be sure, Reiff and his colleagues' views of our secular individualism have largely been engulfed and digested by modern individualism. Does that mean I don't see the value of secular forgiveness? By no means, but at the same time I cannot acknowledge that at its heart, therapeutic forgiveness provides the best and only path to true forgiveness.

What did our canine friend have in mind when he thought about the Nine Steps of forgiveness? The Nine Steps, created by Dr. Fred Luskin and popularized in the early twenty-first century, have become a familiar paradigm for the practice of secular forgiveness. The Nine Steps have become so familiar that they can become the object of humor for a magazine cartoon. Let's take time to reflect on the steps in order that we can grasp what is valued in this particular therapeutic practice of forgiveness. In the First Step, Luskin writes, "Know exactly how you feel about what happened and be able to articulate what about the situation is not OK. Then, tell a trusted couple of people about your experience."[2] Sounds like sensible advice, I should think, provided you accept this view of the human condition. The

2. Luskin, "Forgive for Good."

emphasis clearly falls on the "victim," a topic of which we will have more to say later. Nothing gets said about the perpetrator of the hurt at this point; instead, we're directed to focus on our "feelings." That expression, "feelings," has become so self-validating, so much a part of our modern nomenclature, that we have a hard time getting the objectivity to critique it, but critique it we must. Knowing our "feelings" in the sense that we fully discover who we are, absent our reference to our cultural and social connections, helps us to find our one true self, or so we are led to believe. In truth, knowing exactly what we "feel" has as much to do with our relational context as it does with our individual identity.

The encouragement to discover what's "not OK" about what happened to you makes good sense too but we must ask, by what standards would you know if an apparent offense was OK or not? Once again, our individual interpretation of the offense depends not only on social context but how we remember the injury. For example, if we discover in time that the perpetrator offended unintentionally or out of ignorance, would that be included in our judgment of what's not OK?

Finally, there's truly sound advice in turning to trusted confidants. When we turn to confidants, we add the insights of those social connections of which I spoke earlier. A discerning community can provide us real support and direction. Christians who are active members of a church customarily develop skills for practical faithful living that can only be learned well within a school for faith.

Luskin's third step runs counter to some common theological and philosophical understandings of forgiveness. The step reads: "Forgiveness is for you and not for anyone else." If we were talking about the entire process of forgiveness, on any terms spiritual or philosophical, that statement would be patently absurd. Of course, forgiveness must be about two or more parties—however would there be an offense without both an offender and a victim? But that's not the point Luskin has in mind. What he wants to find for the victim is peace, a peace won by the hard work of "blaming less," "taking the life experience less personally," "and changing your grievance story." In fact, Luskin commendably wants to guide the victim to a therapeutic restoration of a balanced peacefulness. In keeping with modern secular dogma, he would like to have the victim restored to their essential goodness.

Is this a self-serving picture of forgiveness? I should think so. Consider Luskin's Step Eight, where he instructs us to "Remember that a life well lived is your best revenge." "Revenge" would likely not be encouraged in any spiritual direction I know except in the angriest interpretations of faith. But, and this is a very important "but," if you have come to believe that you must cut yourself off from antiquated beliefs, and that you have sought to construct an authentic, self-validating persona, then the tools that Lufkin offers may indeed by the only steps that correspond to your best picture of how to live your life. If these are the tools that fit your lifestyle, then by all means pursue them. Even though I'm inclined to follow a Christian path that values individualism only as an aspect of the Christian life, we are all too aware of the toxic effect of resentments; far better for us to set about living a life well rather than being enslaved to our past hurts.

Americans have long had a strange compulsion to follow steps to success, steps for coping, or steps to understanding. Ben Franklin offered thirteen steps toward "moral perfection," steps that include statements like, "Eat not to dullness; drink not to elevation," or my personal favorite, "Imitate Jesus and Socrates."[3] I find it ironic that we live in a time where politicians and pundits commend the faith of the Founding Fathers and one of the most insightful among them thought Jesus and Socrates belonged on the same shelf! Was Franklin's advice helpful? Yes, provided you agree in the main with his view of success.

Elizabeth Kubler-Ross, through observation of the dying, came up with "the five stages of grief," an invaluable tool for many seeking to understand this ultimate transition. Hewing dogmatically to those steps, however, can cause problems. Those of us who have provided pastoral care know all too well how people caught up in following the defined stages in the proper place can get frustrated when they think they have failed to follow the five stages in order. They wonder if they have somehow fallen short.

The stages of Kubler-Ross and the grieving process can help us see something critical to understanding following steps or stages, or what I prefer to call "following a rule." All of us, without exception, must find ourselves following rules from time to time. We have a whole vast network of rules, for example, devoted to driving. We depend on people following those rules. If a few people in the US suddenly decided of their own accord to follow British driving rules, chaos and death would quickly follow. The example of contrasting British and US driving rules tells us something very important about rule following: our ability to follow rules depends almost entirely on context.

3. Franklin, *Autobiography.*

Over the years, seeking to demonstrate the challenges of rule-following to budding theologians, I have rolled up a piece of a paper into a ball in front of the class. Whe/n I have everyones' attention, I throw the ball to someone in the class. And then I ask, "What should she do with that ball?" People respond, "throw it back," "kick it," or "bat it." The variety of those answers quickly tell the class that whatever game I am playing requires a culture, a context, and a history, and that implies a set of rules. If you know baseball or golf, bridge or even dancing, you know how complex the rules can be, especially if you want to play well. We've got to know the game, a knowledge won by familiarity with our context.

Much the same issues lie at stake in Luskin's Nine Steps. Are they useful? Are the steps valid? Yes, given a certain context and understanding of what it means to be human. Clearly the emphasis in Luskin's "game" falls heavily on the individual and the individual's efforts to create a balanced and peaceful life. Just to make a critical contrast, let me ask how you think Mother Theresa would have dealt with the Nine Steps? I should think that the whole idea of being self-serving would have been at least confusing if not repugnant to her. The saint who sacrificed much for the benefit of others likely would not be persuaded to first take care of herself. My point is that we all live within a community of received practices and commitments; what we wish to do and to some extent, can do with our lives, depends a great deal on our temporal and relational context. We can try to imaginatively separate ourselves from this net of relations, even to the extent of declaring ourselves autonomous individuals, but likely we will not succeed.

Gregory Jones in his book *Embodying Forgiveness: A Theological Analysis* quotes the famous Harvard psychologist Robert Coles regarding our self-absorption in matters of forgiveness: "I wonder whether the deepest mire, the deepest waters of many of America's clergy, not to mention us laymen, may be found in the dreary solipsistic world so many of us have learned to find so interesting: the mind's moods, the various 'stages' and 'phases' of 'human development' or of 'dying,' all dwelt upon (God save us!) as if of Stations of the Cross."[4] Jones and Coles contend that much of what passes for the practice of forgiveness in our time is nothing more than an exercise in psychological therapy. Because this therapy has cut itself off from any rich spiritual tradition except for psychological self-discovery, its sense of the practice of forgiveness makes for thin soup.

4. Jones, *Embodying Forgiveness*, 36.

Jones does think there's a way out of this self-imposed dilemma, a way we'll discuss further in Strand Two. It's worth hearing his summary: "But what if, as the Christian doctrine of sin at its best suggests, one of humanity's most intractable problems is self-deception? And what if, as the Christian practice of embodying forgiveness suggests, we find forgiveness not by looking within ourselves but by being restored to communion with God and with one another in and through specific practices of forgiveness, thus embodying that forgiveness is a way of life?"[5] Jones's theme of the communal sense of forgiveness will become a very important part of our discussion of Strand Two but for the moment, we can appreciate his powerful insight that the way out of self-deception may well be in our forgiving relationship with God and one another.

Not everything I have to say about Strand One focuses on therapeutic forgiveness. In fact, I'd like to turn to the widely accepted process of secular modern forgiveness. Konstan maintains that forgiveness as we think of it today remains a modern creation. The historic picture of forgiveness can be quite different from ours. But what is the modern practice of forgiveness? How does forgiveness progress per our understanding? For the most part, contemporary discussions focus on the interpersonal rather than corporate senses of forgiveness. Bottom line, someone wrongs another person and because of that offense, if the two parties want to continue in relationship, the need for forgiveness follows. For modern forgiveness to progress to the next stage of forgiveness, the wrongdoer must agree with the person wronged that a particular wrong was committed, often understood to be intentionally. After agreeing on the nature of the offense or wrongdoing, the wrongdoer in the next step needs to take responsibility for his or her actions. At this point, or even earlier, the person wronged could go ahead and forgive but most modern accounts of forgiveness disparage this move. Forgiving without the wrongdoer accepting responsibility can be seen as the wronged person's tacit approval of the offense and the offender.

Moving to the next stage. When the offender admits to the wrong and accepts responsibility, modern accounts of forgiveness regard this as the offender taking responsibility for his or her actions. Having done so, the offender is poised to commit to moral change and perhaps even a change in character. Christians call this move "repentance and conversion" but so can the secular sense of forgiveness. Whatever the case, in this last stage the wrongdoer will likely be expected to recompense the wronged for their

5. Jones, *Embodying Forgiveness*, 50.

actions. Simply being forced to repay the wrong doesn't guarantee a sense of moral transformation; that's regarded as one of the weaknesses of the judicial system that even a severe punishment cannot insure reform, let alone regret. Instead, the offender who's undertaken a change of character will demonstrate that the act of forgiveness is truly valid.

I think we could sum up the process something like this: a hurt has been done to the offended. The offended may or may not need to point this out to the offender but when both have acknowledged the offense, forgiveness beyond individual forgiveness can begin. Of course, the wronged can forgive unilaterally; after all, they wish to be freed of their resentments. But if the wrongdoer sincerely regrets his or her injury to the wronged, then the wronged can expect the offender to change, perhaps even to the extent of a lasting change of character. The wrongdoer, having made that commitment to change, can expect that the victim will then forgive them.

Sounds good, doesn't it? Using rational language, we have broken down the process of forgiveness as we appear to use it today into its discrete parts. We train people in this process from our earliest years in school. Preschooler Jane who has hit Bobby over the head with a toy will be required to admit that she's done so. And following that admission, she will need to say she's sorry, even if Jane's only giving lip service. That's how we train people to become adult forgivers, following fundamentally the same action as I outlined above.

While this secular process of forgiveness does not require a spiritual dimension, it certainly recollects the image of the sinner accepting responsibility for sin and committing to repentance and conversion. Nevertheless, and this is very important to secular forgiveness, this process can be undertaken by anyone in any place at any time. This secular forgiveness becomes a kind of tool of practice for modern sociability where we can, offender and offended, learn to live in peace going forward.

There are problems with this secular sense of forgiveness that require our attention. Holes in the perspective, if you will. Returning to our earlier discussion of history, especially as it regards personal memory, we can see that the very nature of what was regarded as an offense by the offended (and perhaps the offender as well) can change. Our emotions can reshape our memory of the injury as well as change our perspectives. One of the weaknesses of the modern sense of forgiveness is that the act of forgiving is often regarded as a once-and-for-all undertaking—that the act of forgiveness occupies the one moment and no other. In this view, forgiveness is a

*what is
never acknowledged.*

once-and-for-all action. Imagine this scenario, though: someone has been deeply hurt by a wrongdoer's actions and words. The wronged have been cut to the core and yet the wrongdoer, when confronted with the offense, refuses to acknowledge its gravity. What's the wronged to do? Simple unilateral forgiveness can feel feeble in circumstances like these.

*new
knowledge
↓*

I spoke with a local law enforcement officer chosen for the job of advocacy for victims, and offender and victim reconciliation. She told me the story of an elderly woman who suffered a home invasion from three heedless teenagers. Following the crime, the offenders had no idea that the woman victim feared every day for their return. The boys had acted on impulse, never planning to victimize the woman again. When the advocate brought the two parties together, the young men were appalled that they had caused the woman so much grief and she in turn was far more forgiving of them having learned how surprised and disappointed they were in themselves. The law officer advocate changed the context, helping both victims and offenders to realize the weight of their actions and bringing some mutual understanding.

me →

Complicating the process, as we can see above, even the wronged can begin to see things differently. The wronged might discover that when the wrongdoer badly hurt them, that the offender was under terrible personal stress. Or similarly, the wronged can come to see that the offender was a juvenile or an addict, two characteristics that will likely temper the wronged person's picture of the gravity of the offense. If the wronged accepts this change of perspective, that doesn't mean that they condone the action but that they see the injury within another context.

We have a similar problem when we look at the very nature of offenses. One of the gifts of modern anthropology has been the insight that cultural context determines the meaning of all our actions, including the nature of our offenses. I've read in Clifford Geertz that the wink we share among friends and partners here in the West, meant to intimate a special connection and to invite a humorous or amorous connection, can invite conflict, even death in North Africa. I was taught in my travels to the Middle East never to put my feet up when I relax, a common practice here at home, or to eat with my left hand. In both cases, the feet and the hand are viewed as symbols of offensive dirt. I noticed in news photos of some of the Middle Eastern dictator's destroyed statues, you will see protestors beating the statue with the soles of their shoes, demonstrating their disgust.

An uninformed viewer out of context wouldn't begin to understand how scorning the protestors' actions were intended to be.

Addiction to alcohol and all the problems associated with that addiction often get treated in very different ways in different cultures. I was taught while serving as a chaplain for a nationally known treatment program that in some countries a second DUI will cause the driver to lose their license for life. Here in the US, a driver, unless you commit a crime under the influence, will in time be reinstated. What's the difference? Cultural convictions lead to different standards of tolerance for behavior.

All of the above point to the notion that an offense is not an offense unless it's regarded as such by the culture and more particularly the community in which the offense was enacted. That means that the forgiveness connected with that offense will shift in meaning too. There's no universal "cookie cutter" approach to the punishment, forgiveness, and possible rehabilitation of offenders. American jails are filled beyond capacity. Some pundits believe it's because of the ill-considered effort to apply broad-based sentencing "guidelines" that were meant to overcome a perceived permissiveness.[6] If this is true, in this case good intentions have gone very much awry.

We don't have to spend much time thinking about how shifting circumstances can swiftly change our perspective on offense and forgiveness. One of my favorite examples comes from the Gospel of John, Chapter 8—the story of the woman caught in adultery. This rich story yields many lessons but for the moment I'll focus on how quickly Jesus can shift the understanding of an offense. The scribes and the Pharisees intended to trip up Jesus with a severe point of the law. They've brought a woman before him caught in adultery (nothing, notably, is said of the partner who would also have been involved in the adultery). Stoning can be the only penalty, the scribes and Pharisees insist, but Jesus suddenly shifts the nature of offense and forgiveness. John reports: "Jesus bent down and wrote with his finger on the ground. When they kept on questioning him, he straightened up and said to them, 'Let anyone among you who is without sin be the first to throw a stone at her.' And once again he bent down and wrote on the ground. When they heard it, they went away, one by one, beginning with the elders; and Jesus was left alone with the woman standing before him. Jesus straightened up and said to her, 'Woman, where are they? Has no one condemned you?' She said, 'No one, sir.' And Jesus said, 'Neither

6. Henning, "White Collar Watch."

do I condemn you. Go your way, and from now on do not sin again."[7] What happened? Has a violation of the law that requires the death penalty been overturned? It turns out that in the mind of Jesus condemnation is not automatically tied to penalties scaled to fit the crime; no sentencing guidelines here. Jesus, by shifting the whole nature of the responsibility for the offense from the individual woman to the corporate guilt of a community has in a strong way changed the very nature of the offense. Adultery becomes not something that others do, an act worthy of punishment, but an occasion for acknowledging our own sins and faults shared with the adulterers, and an opening for forgoing condemnation, an opening that encourages change. All of us need to be reminded that we are disposed to sin even if we are not caught in the act of adultery. Acknowledging that disposition changes our deepest understanding of guilt, punishment, and forgiveness, especially from the heart.

There is another issue yet that has the possibility of undermining the modern secular understanding of forgiveness. If I have been offended and the offender not only acknowledges the offense but further commits to a change of heart, generally we find that satisfies our expectations. But, here's the rub—if the offender commits to change but not does not follow through with the reform, and in fact, falls back into old behaviors, does that invalidate the original forgiveness? Mark Twain provided both a poignant and humorous example of this in his novel, *Huckleberry Finn*. Huck's father, Pap, is a notorious drunkard and troublemaker. Pap, faced with punishment for his behavior, declares to the clergy and all that will believe him that he has been saved and is now a new man, cleansed of his old self. Everyone's happy except for Huck who, based on experience, suspects Pap's sincerity. Sure enough, sometime later, Pap gets drunk and falls off the roof of a house, breaking his leg. The clergy who have forgiven him are up in arms; we must wonder if there can be lasting forgiveness from the clergy or anyone else for characters like these.

That's not a small question but a large one representing the sorts of issues with which we'll wrestle in the forthcoming Strand Two forgiveness. In Strand One, secular forgiveness, much of the emphasis falls on the benefit of forgiveness for the offended. We want to be relieved of a burden of resentment that can cripple our psyche. That's not the only issue in Strand One—as we can see, finding appropriate punishment to expunge the guilt

7. John 8: 1–11.

70

of the offender plays an important part. And indeed, in some cases, pursuing reconciliation can be one of the desired outcomes.

The reader might get the idea that I do not value Strand One forgiveness but that would not be the case. Absent the religious convictions that can underpin forgiveness and in fact, shape the character of the forgiver, secular forgiveness will do our world well. I am troubled by the secularization of our culture but it's a force, even a tectonic movement, that has shifted us from a culture of relationship with God and one another to an exceptionally strong valuing of the individual above all associations.[8] Howsoever the rise of the secular and the therapeutic might be stated, I believe at its core, forgiveness relies on the image of ecclesial and finally the divine act of forgiveness. The church has by its nature developed separately from the secular while still reflecting secular elements in its practices. But I don't believe the opposite is true—secular forgiveness relies heavily on the pattern of ecclesiastical forgiveness. I believe the divine impulse to forgive, unconditionally and as a gift, forms the core of forgiveness.   *yes!,*

8. The Canadian philosopher Charles Taylor has made the case in *A Secular Age* for the complicated forces involved.

6

Strand Two Forgiveness:
The Church at Work in the World

EARLIER, WE LOOKED AT forgiveness largely with respect to its effect on individuals, a kind of forgiveness that seeks to bring hope and change largely for just the offended. Strand One can be seen in many ways (though by no means the only ways) as therapeutic when founded on setting right the spirit, the mind, and the heart of the individual. We, as individuals, want to be healthy and integrated of mind and spirit.

Strand Two forgiveness is more about community, and to my chief interest, more particularly, about the church community, the ecclesia. Strand Two forgiveness brings us the hope of reconciliation, atonement (at-one-ment), and with that reconciliation, the hope of seeing one another as valuable creations, even magnificent creations in the eyes of the creator. I recognize that these three strands often overlap, intermingling with one another. In a sense, talk of three strands might seem artificial, even arbitrary; who after all could separate the three strands of forgiveness in daily life? But my purpose here is to move people to embrace forgiveness as a way of life. Perhaps your picture of forgiveness comes with a wish to embrace forgiveness so that you as an individual can be at peace with the world. Good. But forgiveness that is initiated, expressed, and practiced in community can bring people, even the entire creation, together in mutual respect and perhaps even love.

To that end, Strand Two represents forgiveness from three viewpoints. They are by no means the only ways we may speak of Strand Two forgiveness but they all profit us by encouraging us to embrace communal forgiveness.

First, there is power in real-world stories to help us to understand forgiveness. Over the course of my ministry, I've had people say to me many times, "Well, that's a great ideal, Jeff, but those kinds of Christian ideals won't work in the 'real world.'" I have a serious objection with that sense of the term *real*, for what could be more real than God and God's creation? I want to tell you stories of real-world encounters with forgiveness, and that forgiveness not only can but does indeed work. We'll look most closely at the work of Desmond Tutu and we will listen to the stories of a minister of the gospel in the aftermath of the Tutsi-Hutu conflict. Forgiveness of the Strand Two variety may not seem workably "real" to some people, but I think that's because what we will explore has been so rarely practiced.

Second, we will also look at the eschatological understanding of forgiveness, that is, how forgiveness might affect the end of time. Why is that so important? Because for the clear majority of Christians, and other religious believers too, the end of time, the final revealing of God's purpose, is also understood to be a time of judgment, a time when we are held accountable for our past. How we understand that judgment matters a great deal to how we should live our life in this world today. We'll turn to several figures to help us understand this perspective, including L. Gregory Jones and Miroslav Volf, the latter of which has some poignant real-world stories to tell, and we'll look too to the author Flannery O'Connor and how one of her short stories reveals even more subtly the impact of judgment. Also, we'll turn to the witness of Dom Christian de Chergé, one of several French Algerian monks martyred by Muslim radicals. Dom Christian witnesses to a forgiveness during judgment that seems impossible to refute. Let me be clear: end-of-time judgments are not restricted to the religious—secular people think in those terms as well, especially in the light of nuclear threat, climate change, and the like—but for the most part, I will focus on the eschaton of the religious.

And then last, I will share one of the most remarkable stories of church communal forgiveness I know, the story of the aftermath of the terrible murders of the girls at the Amish Nickel Mine school and how the Old Order Amish responded with deep and costly forgiveness. The Old Order Amish's radical forgiveness became an object of admiration to many, of an impulse to imitate their forgiveness by some, but also the focus of disdain and even anger for a few.

I will conclude this section by offering a theological discussion of the atonement. Talk of Christ's atonement has often fallen fallow in modern times but that doesn't mean it isn't important. Some people have rejected some notions of what Jesus effected on the cross as too bloody minded or too legalistic. There's some truth in the criticism of both, depending on how they are portrayed, but more misunderstanding as well. In the end, I hope to show you how the work of the cross, how the suffering, death, and resurrection of Jesus became the hinge of history so that everything, literally everything in the universe, turned towards forgiveness.

Desmond Tutu and Celestin Musekura: Stories of Forgiveness and Reconciliation

Desmond Tutu may be one of the most beloved figures of the late twentieth and early twenty-first centuries. And with just cause—Tutu has won recognition and prizes, including the Nobel Peace Prize, and despite these manifold honors, remains a humble and loving man of faith. I've had the joy of spending time with him on several occasions and have never come away from listening to him without being both uplifted and challenged. You cannot but feel while in Bishop Tutu's presence that you are for the moment the most important person in the archbishop's life. I think I could fairly say that a large measure of Archbishop Tutu's life work has been the practice of forgiveness. Since Tutu grew up amidst apartheid and its horrors, this must come as no surprise. (I heard the archbishop say in a small discussion one time that the word "apartheid" should always be pronounced, "apart-hate!") I believe that as the decades go by, his part in the establishment of the Truth and Reconciliation Commission in South Africa will be regarded as a high point of human achievement.

Earlier I remarked how much our expectations of how forgiveness works are shaped by our cultural context. The archbishop mines his South African sense of context for meanings that can illuminate our own Western concerns. Early in his and his daughter Mpho's book, *The Book of Forgiving*,[1] Tutu writes about how the people of South Africa view their world: "In South Africa, *Ubuntu* is our way of making sense of the world. The word literally means 'humanity.' It is the philosophy and belief that a person is only a person through other people. In other words, we are only human in our relation to other humans . . . . Our humanity is bound up in one another, and any tear in the fabric of connection between us

1. Tutu and Tutu, *The Book of Forgiving*.

must be repaired for us all to be made whole."[2] *Ubuntu* has so grasped our imagination that "*ubuntu*" became the guiding theme of a recent meeting of the General Convention of the Episcopal Church, and the idea of *ubuntu* has been so engaging that even a popular open-source computer operating system is named the same!

Let's take a moment to compare the Strand One and Strand Two approaches to forgiveness: were we to imagine human relationships as a web, in Strand One the individual would lie at the center of the web of concerns. In Strand One all paths lead back to "me." In Strand Two, the image of the web continues but this time rather than lying at the center of the web, the person is part of a larger network of persons, and the very connections between those persons defines the person among related persons. Very different approaches, very different outcomes. In Strand One, we look for forgiveness to relieve the burden of resentments for the individual, to set the person free to find their value. In Strand Two, we find our freedom and our value in our ties to one another. In Strand Two, offenses between parties ruptured by hurt or sin need to be healed and forgiveness becomes the means.

To be sure, Tutu does say at one point that the purpose of forgiveness is to forgive ourselves but his approach to forgiveness chiefly focuses on the Other, the person not ourselves who may in no way share our values. Tutu makes many of his strongest points by telling stories, some of them quite personal. In fact, of the four steps[3] that the Tutus identify as the path to forgiveness, telling truthfully the story of the hurt comes first. How important is this storytelling? The Tutus wrote: "In writing this book, we consulted with many of the leading experts on forgiveness around the world . . . . Every one of them said how important it is to be able to tell a new story and how this ability is a sign of healing and wholeness . . . . Your story is no longer just about the facts of what happened, or about the pain and hurt your suffered. It is a story that recognizes the story of the one who hurt you . . . . It is a story that recognizes our common humanity."[4]

Why does storytelling benefit forgiveness? Because telling a story allows both the perpetrator and the victim to tell how they became the people

---

2. Tutu and Tutu, *The Book of Forgiving*, 9.

3. The four are: 1. Telling the Story, 2. Naming the Hurt, 3. Granting Forgiveness, and 4. Renewing or Releasing the relationship. See Merritt, "Desmond Tutu's four steps to forgiving others."

4. Tutu and Tutu, *The Book of Forgiving*, 133.

they are (rather than simply pointing to the hurt or sin taken out of context). Alcoholics Anonymous has a similar move in its Twelves Steps, the Fifth Step, where the recovering person must tell their story and learn to tell it truthfully. When we hear someone's story we come to realize how richly nuanced every person's moral development is. As I pointed our earlier, forgiveness might well come easier if we see the offender embedded in their *ubuntu*, especially if that network of relationship comes from a fundamentally unhealthy history. Some years ago, I spent time with a priest who had his privileges revoked because of a divorce. His experience had been messy and troubling but now, after a decade or more, he wished to be reinstated. I spent some time unpacking his history and discovered that his former wife had been alcoholic and drug addicted, a fact he had attempted to hide, and a fact that contributed more misery to his divorce. Having heard him out, I advocated for his reinstatement with our bishop. Granted the divorce had been public and painful but his character and the character of his offense took on different shadings in the context of his history. Shortly thereafter, he was reinstated to holy orders.

The Tutus' point goes even further—if the victim and the offender can agree on a truthful narrative of the crime, then healing can begin. Until we can agree on the offense, the "revenge cycle," as the Tutus call it, operates open-ended while we try to find the fair and equitable justice. Perhaps that's the greatest power of the Truth and Reconciliation Commission, that they could expose the truth to the light to let the healing begin.

Of particular interest, Bishop Tutu writes of unconditional forgiveness, a forgiveness that frees the victim and the offender: "Unconditional forgiveness is a different model of forgiveness than the gift with strings. This is forgiveness as a grace, a free gift freely given. In this model, forgiveness frees the person who inflicted the harm from the weight of the victim's whim—what the victim may demand in order to grant forgiveness—and the victim's threat of vengeance."[5] Notice that there's little room for individuals' concerns in this kind of unconditional forgiveness. Indeed, the truly powerful insight is that the perpetrator is freed from the whim of the victim. As many forms of forgiveness are conditional in our world, it's sometimes hard to grasp Tutu's point. Most felons in the US are not fully pardoned but released with conditions to parole. Many parolees tell stories of suffering at the whim of the courts and others until they had finally served their entire punishment. Similar behaviors can take place interpersonally or within a

5. Tutu and Tutu, *The Book of Forgiving*, 21.

community. How many spouses have suffered a conditional forgiveness, governed by the whims of their angry spouse? Imagine then if we think of ourselves as someone who has offended God; wouldn't total and unconditional forgiveness be a complete grace, a complete gift? We would be free of any supposed "whim" of God that might threaten our lives.

The Tutus make one more important point: forgiveness is a skill, a practice, and a matter of character, and like all skills, can be developed over time. Like bricklaying or chess, baking or skiing, where regular and repeated efforts make for better and more proficient outcomes, so too in a more important way with forgiveness. The Tutus write, "The repeated exercise of forgiveness, offered in small ways, means that a pattern is already in place when, or if, one must confront an unspeakable need."[6] The ability to forgive is not something that we can summon up willy-nilly, even if we devoutly admire persons who practice forgiveness, but must be a developed skill. I suspect that people in lasting relationships who take forgiveness seriously, as in marriage or friendship, for example, have already established a strong and lasting foundation for forgiveness in times of duress. They've found themselves practicing forgiveness in small and large ways alike. I'm told by psychologist friends who practice marriage therapy that there is as much conflict in good marriages as in bad, but that the good marriages have become skilled in forgiving.

In 100 days during the spring and summer of 1994, as many as a million Tutsis and Hutus died in a slaughter incited and encouraged by the Hutu government of Rwanda. The slaughter was so horrific that the world stood back in revulsion; how could something so impossibly ferocious occur? Who could possibly hold these murderers accountable? The problem in summoning up an appropriate punishment was something that Hannah Arendt considered with regards to the Holocaust—who could possibly conceive of a punishment to fit the Nazi crime? We can weigh Arendt's remarks when regarding the Hutu-Tutsi genocide; what's the appropriate punishment for as many as a million slaughtered? A further issue exacerbated the healing; the coercion brought to bear on moderate Hutus to participate in the slaughter was enormous—if they failed to join in, they too would suffer the fate of their neighbor Tutsis. To say that such Hutus were accountable would be true but not in the same way, surely, as the guilty Hutu government officials that instigated the slaughter.

6. Tutu and Tutu, *The Book of Forgiving*, 119

Some people in the West were under the impression that this was a Muslim and Christian conflict, but that was not the case. Indeed, to compound the horror to some Western minds, both Hutu and Tutsis counted themselves as Christian. Christians were killing Christians for nothing more nor less than racist hate. Celestin Musekura and Gregory Jones joined in writing a remarkable book entitled *Forgiving as We Have Been Forgiven*.[7] As in the Tutus' book on forgiveness, Musekura and Jones have focused on the communal practices of forgiveness and what makes that forgiveness possible. In fact, the subtitle of Musekura and Jones's book is *Community Practices for Making Peace*.

I was particularly struck by Pastor Musekura's account of his acts of forgiveness and refusal to take vengeance despite the loss of his own parishioners and family members. I suspect many of us would bend and break under the weight of the horror but Musekura, summoning his faith, wrote: "It was not my responsibility to question where God was when they were killed and who killed them, but rather to finish the journey well like both my family and other faithful church members who were killed during and after the genocide."[8] Unlike so many people I've met in the West, Pastor Musekura's path to forgiveness did not begin with recriminations against God—how could God permit something so horrible?—but instead in recognizing that people killed people, not God. Further, and this was the pastor's resolve, if Musekura wished to honor the faith of his parishioners and family members, he needed to find a way to forgive.

But how should he forgive? How could he forgive? To my wonder, Musekura spoke of God's "unconditional forgiveness." I cannot emphasize enough Musekura's move to unconditional forgiveness—if you had seen nearly a million people slaughtered including your family and friends, could you speak in terms of the "unconditional"? And yet Musekura did.

Where did Musekura get the idea of "unconditional forgiveness"? The pastor wrote: "He made us alive with Christ even when we were powerless and dead through our transgressions (Ephesians 2:5; Romans 5:6–8). Because of this divine act, the Christian model of forgiveness stresses the grant of unconditional forgiveness to those who cause injury, pain and suffering in this life."[9] Here we have arrived at a key insight of Musekura's—rather than blame the Hutu and hold them singularly guilty, Musekura takes Saint

7. Musekura and Jones, *Forgiving as We've Been Forgiven*.

8. Musekura and Jones, *Forgiving as We've Been Forgiven*, 21.

9. Musekura and Jones, *Forgiving as We've Been Forgiven*, 22.

Paul's verses to heart—we are all powerless, we are all dead through our transgressions. In other words, all people, Hutu, Tutsi, we ourselves, live in the shadow of death. While it would be certainly true that some are guiltier than others, Musekura contends that communally we are all together, equally dead in our transgressions; more, for this is very important, that we are powerless to effect our own salvation, let alone our own forgiveness.[10]

I suspect Musekura's notion that we are powerless would fly in the face of Western perceptions, especially for those of us caught up in a more therapeutic picture of humanity. Some people who believe they can save themselves by seeking self-actualization; for them, Musekura's claim of powerlessness would sound hollow. On reflection, many of us might come down on Musekura's side. After all, if we only must be self-actualized to be saved from our offenses then how can we explain that we continue to wrestle with the horrors of Hitler and Pol Pot? Why didn't humanity rise in howling protest? I think the flow of history tends to support Musekura and not the therapeutic. Pastor Musekura wrote, "We need something more than therapeutic self-help. The uniqueness of Christian forgiveness derives from its motivation in divine forgiveness and its practice modeled by and within the community of believers."[11]

Musekura's remarkable stories of forgiveness are many; I urge you to read them. His account of forgiveness is far from merely conceptual. Instead it is based in real encounters with real people, including other pastors who supported the slaughter. Some of the offenders Musekura met were less than penitent, still others apparently penitent but in fact, insincere. But unlike many modern accounts of the steps of forgiveness, Musekura did not feel he had the time or authority to delay forgiveness until the criminals repented. Instead he wrote, "God was teaching me that I can choose to forgive regardless of the actions of the offender. I don't have to completely heal from wounds before I forgive. The gift doesn't even have to be received to be a gift. Forgiveness is the gift that I have freely received and that I should unconditionally give."[12] Musekura's reflections have contributed to the main message of my Strand Three, that God initiates forgiveness unconditionally. What I'm struck by in the pastor's account of forgiving is that while the struggle to forgive some of these heinous and cowardly criminals was

10. Pastor Musekura's sense of "unconditional forgiveness" anticipates some of what I will discuss in the Third Strand.

11. Musekura and Jones, *Forgiving as We've Been Forgiven*, 29.

12. Musekura and Jones, *Forgiving as We've Been Forgiven*, 24.

deeply difficult, Musekura felt he had no other choice but to forgive—after all, as a member of the greater community of Rwanda and the world, he too had already been forgiven by the power of the cross.

Musekura summarizes his views on the need and power of forgiveness: "In the prayer Jesus taught his disciples to pray, he emphasized the daily practice of forgiveness as a way of maintaining and sustaining relationships. Just like food, forgiveness sustains our lives in the community. Just as we cannot live without our daily bread, we cannot fully live our life in communion with each other and with God without the ability to grant and receive forgiveness (Matthew 6:9–15)."[13] Just like the Tutus, Pastor Musekura asserts that if we want to become skilled at forgiveness, perhaps even our own, then we must seek to forgive continually until we begin to practice forgiving as the skill it is. And that's not all—while many people would surely contend that the love, charity, and respect are the cornerstones of community, Musekura feels that the practice of forgiveness is just as important. In other words, we are as much bonded as human beings by forgiveness as we are by agape, the sacrificial love that Jesus calls us to—and indeed, perhaps love and forgiveness are all of a piece.

There is one more remarkable true story of forgiveness, a story born not in the abstract nor the conceptual but instead founded in the reality of responding to hate through martyrdom. Some of you may know the story of Dom Christian de Chergé either through reading or because of a remarkable film about his life and the life of his fellow monks, *Of Gods and Men*.[14] Near the end of March 1996, seven Trappist monks, including the Dom, were kidnapped and later murdered by political extremists during the Algerian civil war. Notably, the Trappists, long warned both by the extremists and the authorities, could have run to save themselves. But like the Christ they sought to emulate, the monks elected to stay and they paid with their lives.

Recognizing that their martyrdom might be at hand, Dom Christian wrote a letter to family and friends. Dom Christian wrote, "If it should happen one day—and it could be today—that I become a victim of the terrorism which now seems ready to engulf all the foreigners living in Algeria, I would like my community, my Church and my family to remember that my life was GIVEN to God and to this country."[15] Faced with his death and

13. Musekura and Jones, *Forgiving as We've Been Forgiven*, 28.

14. Martin, "Brother Christian's Testament."

15. Martin, "Brother Christian's Testament."

the death of his fellow monks, Dom Christian declared that in no way could his life be "taken" from him but should only be understood as "given" in service to God. The Dom continued in terms now familiar to us from the Tutus and Pastor Musekura: "I have lived long enough to know that I am an accomplice in the evil which seems to prevail so terribly in the world, even in the evil which might blindly strike me down." Like those I've cited before, even the Trappist recognizes that we cannot be in this world without being part of injuring the world, especially the part that needs and requires forgiveness. As humanity, we are a community of the powerless who has a desperate need to learn to forgive as Christ forgave. Finally, Dom Christian writes, "I should like, when the time comes, to have a moment of spiritual clarity which would allow me to beg forgiveness of God and of my fellow human beings, and at the same time forgive with all my heart the one who would strike me down." Here, Dom Christian makes a summary statement much like that of which we've read above—we are as much a community by need of forgiveness as we are community shaped by love and mercy. Dom Christian only asks this, that by his witness, he would have the power to forgive, much as Christ forgave on the cross, the ones who kill him. God forgive them, for they don't know what they are doing.

Jones and Eschatological Judgment

Impressive word, *eschatological*, but what does it signify? Eschatological, which derives from the Greek word *eschaton*, refers to the end of time, the point of intersection where the ultimate purpose of God for creation and time come together in fulfillment. Very commonly, when we talk about the eschaton, we're also talking about judgment, the weighing out of human sin and goodness, and the consequent reward or punishment humanity suffers, follows from that judgment.

Talk of the eschaton and of judgment make for a slippery slope. Most people come to the discussion with a predisposed idea of heaven and hell with the former a reward for a good life, the latter an eternal punishment. Many people sense rightly that there's something askew with the picture of heaven and hell as eternal rewards for God's judgment. While we may find it hard to put into words, the idea that there's some sort of legal formula (like some type of divine sentencing guidelines) for reward and punishment appears terribly arbitrary. I was brought up in an evangelical household and one of the confusing convictions I experienced was the notion that the punishment for stealing a candy bar and a car were roughly equal. Both merited a sentence to hell. I found that agonizingly disturbing for my youthful mind. Mind you, the very notion of hewing to the good to gain eternal reward goes back generations into my Appalachian background. But the stark sense of eternal reward that encouraged both hope and fear for those working in the deep darkness of the coal mine, as my grandfather did, did not serve me well as a small child in suburban Minneapolis. Fear of punishment doesn't automatically serve up good behavior, whatever "good" might mean. But not all judgment has the same outcome; later, we'll turn to a short story of Flannery O'Connor that welcomes judgment, but you'll read that judgment might not be prejudicial but in fact is a kind of reward for everyone.

Humanity brings its own perception of law and justice to the whole notion of the eschaton. Truth is, we as a human community find it very difficult to imagine that there's any other outcome to judgment; there must be a time when the good should be rewarded and the evil must necessarily get their just desserts! The caution inherent in that view of judgment will become clear when we talk about forms of atonement, one form of which contends that Jesus died on the cross to satisfy legal requirements, laws of reward and punishment, that even God cannot ignore. Over the years, I've had many people ask me if God can forgive Hitler. In every case, it seems, the people questioning had in mind a legal sense of judgment at the end of time; if God were to obey what appear to be God's laws, how could God forgive sins so heinous? It's by no means a small question but in many ways, the question speaks more to the human sense of the limits of judgment than it does to God's.

I don't think we can simply ignore judgment, a central issue to forgiveness; apparently, Jesus takes the talk of end times very seriously, especially when he talks about those who will be judged and thrown into the eternal fire (the Gospel of Matthew alone talks about hell six times). When Jesus speaks of the end times, he's looking to a time when all the wrongs of this world will be set right and justice, the kingdom of God's justice, will prevail. If our focus on God's judgment only looks to the eschaton as a future point in time, God's judgment does have limits. But if the judgment of the eschaton reflects back from the end of time into our daily lives, we have a different sense of judgment. If we know a time of judgment is coming, we have the means and the insight to live our lives differently considering that judgment day. Much as a driver might be warned of a fallen bridge ahead and then take another road, so too with the offender who is warned of a judgment to come can take another path. A very important question follows: does Jesus mean for this sense of judgment to affect only the life to come or does he mean to bring change into this life as well?

Is then talk of the eschaton simply judgmental? Are our lives to be weighed in the balance and that's that? Gregory Jones and his remarkable book, *Embodying Forgiveness*,[16] can help us find our way. Jones formerly made the point, in the book he wrote with Pastor Musekura, that the eschaton provides the opportunity for the "healing of memories." Jones has more in mind when he writes this than simply being relieved of our resentments, something the individual can do alone. Jones believes that if we want to be healed of memories, that healing requires the intervention of God in Jesus Christ.

Some might well ask, "Why not just forget the past and put the evil of those who have injured us behind us?" In Jones's view, if we simply forget the past, "let bygones be bygones" no matter how evil those bygones might have been, then we have ignored the lasting horror such actions may have inflicted on the injured. As Jones writes, "erasing memories would seem to 'uncrucify' Christ rather than heal those memories fully—eschatologically—through the healing wounds of the crucified and risen Christ."[17] In other words, Christ went to the cross in large part for healing our terrible wounds; if we just ignore those wounds, as if the insult never happened, not only have we "uncrucified" Christ we have also denied justice both to the victim *and* the perpetrator. In this arrangement, the victim's pain will be ignored and the perpetrator will have no reason to change if we forego the possibility of eschatological judgement.

Those last points should remind us once again that humanity lives under its own rules of justice and law. Theologians have sought to strike a balance between divine law and human law in several ways; Augustine wrote about the City of God and the City of Man, where the City of God reflected God's values. Luther spoke of two Kingdoms, one of heaven and one of earth, each having its own scope of influence. Humanity owes fealty to both God and human law in Luther's scheme. It may seem strange to think human and divine law might be in conflict. But let's speak of some of the incommensurate rules observed just in human law. Perfectly reasonable people in another part of the world believe that they should conduct their

16. Jones, *Embodying Forgiveness*.

17. Jones, *Embodying Forgiveness*, 98.

lives under Sharia, a law reflecting Islamic religious principles, while at the same time people in the West, equally reasonable, find Sharia troubling. Some Westerners, who have been persuaded that there should be a separation of church and state, might well wonder, what's religion doing shaping social laws? Who is right? One of the problems all humans face is the not uncommon sense that if we drill down deep enough into our respective convictions, we'll find a common ground and universal law. We've been looking for such a common foundation for over 2,500 years and the common ground continues to and will likely always elude us.

Accountability may be the greatest issue regarding judgement, at least pertaining to the perpetrator. Not many of us have witnessed a criminal change of their own volition. How many of us have seen someone evil spontaneously convert from bad intentions to good? We rightly observe that people's behavior sometimes can be governed and even changed when confronted by the threat of judgment. But not always and not under every circumstance. The threat of punishment doesn't stop every child from stealing from a neighbor's unattended apple tree. In a strong analogy, neither does the threat of the death penalty stop people from heinous crimes. The fact that people continue to murder despite the threat of the death penalty should tell us something—accountability only matters to some people in some circumstances. Those who advocate for the death penalty as a deterrent have likely ignored the daily news.

Studying our actions and commitments while considering the eschaton can bring an enormous weight of accountability to bear on the present. If there's a judgment at the end of time, we might well think that the possibility of judgment would cause people to change. The New Testament can shed some new light on how we think about this. The story of the rich man and Lazarus will be very telling. Here is the story from the Gospel of Luke:

> There was a rich man who was dressed in purple and fine linen and who feasted sumptuously every day. 20 And at his gate lay a poor man named Lazarus, covered with sores, 21 who longed to satisfy his hunger with what fell from the rich man's table; even the dogs would come and lick his sores. 22 The poor man died and was carried away by the angels to be with Abraham. The rich man also died and was buried. 23 In Hades, where he was being tormented, he looked up and saw Abraham far away with Lazarus by his side. 24 He called out, "Father Abraham, have mercy on me, and send Lazarus to dip the tip of his finger in water and cool my tongue; for I am in agony in these flames." 25 But Abraham said,

"Child, remember that during your lifetime you received your good things, and Lazarus in like manner evil things; but now he is comforted here, and you are in agony. 26 Besides all this, between you and us a great chasm has been fixed, so that those who might want to pass from here to you cannot do so, and no one can cross from there to us." 27 He said, "Then, father, I beg you to send him to my father's house— 28 for I have five brothers—that he may warn them, so that they will not also come into this place of torment." 29 Abraham replied, "They have Moses and the prophets; they should listen to them." 30 He said, "No, father Abraham; but if someone goes to them from the dead, they will repent." 31 He said to him, "If they do not listen to Moses and the prophets, neither will they be convinced even if someone rises from the dead." (Luke 16:19–31, NRSV)

This incredibly rich story serves to illustrate several points relevant to this discussion. This story wasn't written particularly for either the rich man's or Lazarus's benefit, it was told for the benefit of the listening crowd and written down for us. This story was meant as a caution and an encouragement to change. It's a caution as it stands to those who are wealthy and do not give justice and charity to the poor. In that sense, the story is a form of encouragement to the rich and powerful: when we look backwards in time from the vantage of the eschaton, we are called to change now, change the things of this world now, and in this present-day world to practice the values of the kingdom of God. So, the story serves two purposes for us, as a cautionary tale and to urge us to make changes that reflect God's good desires for all people.

There's a further point to consider. Jesus, telling this story, takes the punishment of Hades very seriously. The rich man's failure to give provision to Lazarus has left the rich man nameless and alone in eternal punishment. The rich man, as you can read, is nameless while the poor man will always be remembered by the name Lazarus. Further, as the story is told, even Abraham cannot ignore the imposed judgment to bring comfort to the nameless rich man. The eschatological implications are driven home in a very powerful way when the rich man asks Abraham to send a warning to his five brothers. Abraham demurs, asserting that the brothers already have Moses and the prophets—they should listen to them. Then the rich man says that if someone appeared to the brothers from the dead, they would surely listen. Anticipating all of those who will not take the judgment of the eschaton with the utmost seriousness, Abraham responds, "If they do not listen to Moses and the prophets, neither will they be convinced even if someone rises from the dead."

I think that we can interpret that last line in at least two ways with respect to forgiveness. It could be that God in Jesus Christ is simply condemning all those to eternal perdition who fail to listen to the Scriptures and act on them. But if that were the case and the coming judgment already eternally fixed, what then does Jesus mean to accomplish by telling this story? Surely God's prejudicial judgment cannot be regarded as indelible. Instead, if we should listen to this story and act on it now, in this world and in this life, forgiveness can still be given. Rather than concluding with the horror of a divine predestination to eternal punishment, I believe the story concludes with the gift of hope delivered by the contemplation of the eschaton.

As we can see, the eschaton can deliver both judgment as accountability, and hope in the strong sense that if we look to the coming accounting, we can change our lives to reflect the values of the kingdom of God. Accountability can become a gracious gift to us, not a liability.

Jones repeatedly makes the point that forgiveness is not just about the individual but involves the entire community. Jones wrote, "Forgiveness aims to restore communion on the part of humans with God, with one another, and with the whole of creation."[18] Here's a critical point for all believers—insofar as we are called into forgiveness, we are called into the presence of God. From the Christian vantage, all acts of forgiveness are at least a three-way relationship, between the victim, the perpetrator, and God.

Why does Strand Two emphasize community over the individual? Because Strand Two holds that when we are broken in spirit and by sin, we are not alone—we are part of a great community of people, all of whom share in brokenness and sin. Of course, not everyone believes brokenness and sin to be the character of humanity, but many Christians do. Secularists may conclude that society suffers from broken relations for many reasons including intrinsic injustice, financial inequality, racism, and similar issues. Christians often accept the secularist view, but also believe that we are often broken in relationship with one another. Because of those broken relationships, we have a broken relationship with God. Remember the greatest commandment, to love God and your neighbor as yourself. Loving along with forgiveness heals broken relationships. We can see this restoration

18. Jones, *Embodying Forgiveness*, 163.

of relationship at work in the Eucharist, according to Jones, who wrote, "Forgiveness aims to restore communion on the part of humans with God, with one another, and with the whole of creation."[19] The word *Eucharist* comes from the Greek word for thanksgiving. Thanksgiving for the bread and wine, the body and blood that Christ gave us. Thanksgiving for the restoration of relationship initiated by God. Thanksgiving for the community of Christians formed by the Eucharist.

The offering of the Eucharist began with the last meal Jesus shared with his disciples, a Passover meal recollecting God sparing Israel while providing an escape from slavery in Egypt. This time God, in the meal Christ provided, means to free humanity from the slavery of death. The cross and the resurrection together grant us what we call "atonement," an atonement that leads to that freedom. Because forgiveness is necessarily a communal activity in the Christian tradition, this healing that leads to "at-one-ment" plays a critical part in restoring us to one another, even reconciling us to one another, the creation, and to the Trinity. In Strand Two, forgiveness and atonement are part and parcel of one another.

How are we to gain this forgiveness? Many Christians believe that as humanity, we don't gain forgiveness by our own initiative but by God's intervention in the cross. This take on forgiveness does not diminish the need for the healing of individual's resentments, but the initiative and the power to forgive and heal the threefold community of victim, perpetrator, and God, come from Christ and the cross. Is this the unconditional forgiveness of which I spoke earlier? In part. Jones maintains that "there are no conditions for God forgiving us," but "we must engage in practices of repentance in order to appropriate that forgiveness. That is to say, God's forgiveness becomes available to us as we learn to see both the reality of the world under judgement and our participation in that fallenness."[20]

What does Jones mean by "engage in practices of repentance"? Yes, God unconditionally forgives. In fact, citing his friend and fellow theologian, Stanley Hauerwas, Jones agrees that we as Christians are "already forgiven," forgiven before we ask. But, and this is critical, there is a response to that forgiveness that Jones believes signals the guarantee we have been forgiven—we must see the brokenness of the world and own up to our contribution to that brokenness. Paralleling Konstan's steps of forgiveness, we must own our fault, and then we can accept God's forgiveness through

19. Jones, *Embodying Forgiveness*, 176.
20. Jones, *Embodying Forgiveness*, 146.

repentance. If this process appears similar the contemporary understanding of secular forgiveness, it is because it is. The steps are there, including a form of shared recognition of the evil done and the perpetrator owning the evil and desiring to change. We call that desire to change "conversion" in the church.

Jones's *Embodying Forgiveness* sets a high bar in its contribution to discussions of forgiveness. The book may be the most comprehensive contribution to the discussion of Christian forgiveness in the last thirty years. And yet, I want to draw your attention to Jones's requirement that "we must engage in practices of repentance in order to appropriate that forgiveness." Not all philosophers and theologians will agree—in the minds of a few, forgiveness is a kind of gift and as a gift, it does not require that it must be appropriated to still be called a gift. Another slippery slope? To be sure. How can we know if someone has been forgiven if there's no change in the offender's character? We can pose important questions: if we are forgiven completely and unconditionally, how could we appropriate such an immense gift? Wouldn't such an enormous gift of forgiveness be beyond our human grasp? If God forgives us completely and unilaterally, how could we possibly comprehend the breadth and depth of that forgiveness?

Sometimes talk about forgiveness can be so recursive and complex that the conversation folds back on itself. As an example, how can we know what God's forgiveness is if we ourselves can scarcely conceive of such a divine forgiveness? More even, we must wonder how we could be expected to emulate it. That's where stories become very important; if we can imagine something, perhaps what we imagine may occur.

American authors have had a long, profound dialogue with the Christian faith, authors as diverse as Hawthorne and Melville, Walker Percy and Wendell Berry. But among the most celebrated may be Flannery O'Connor, a writer who throws our inmost faith convictions into dark but comic high relief. O'Connor's short stories and novels have continued to provide theological insight into our most important faith practices, including the practice of forgiveness.

One of O'Connor's short stories, entitled "Revelation," has become a favorite of many Christians, including Gregory Jones. During the story, we're introduced to a Mrs. Ruby Turpin, a largely self-satisfied and most self-righteous person. She's married to silent, comical Claude, a man of middling success in his community. The story begins with Ruby and Claude visiting a doctor's office, where in the waiting room they meet all kinds of people from her town, people of different social strata and races. The behavior of these people both appalls and confirms Ruby's suspicions about those she believes lie lower than she in the laddered order of the universe—people like "white trash" and African Americans. One person sees through Ruby's veil of sanctimony, a young Wellesley student who in short order discovers she cannot abide Ruby. Unhinged though the student is, plainly she gets the true picture of Ruby that Ruby's self-regard doesn't permit. When the Wellesley student can no longer stand Ruby a moment longer, she throws a book at her and then leaps to strangle Ruby. In the ensuing tangle, just as Ruby hopes to be generous towards the young woman, the girl hisses that Ruby is a warty "hog."

This encounter shocks Ruby and pierces the fog of self-satisfaction that envelops her; she struggles afterward with her feelings. As the day comes to an end, she wanders down to the corner of the farm where Claude's pigs are kept in a "parlor." Staring towards the red glare of the sun setting over the pig parlor, "Mrs. Turpin remained there with her gaze bent to them as if she were absorbing some abysmal life-giving knowledge."[21] When Ruby lifted her head, she saw a purple streak across the sky, like a highway running from earth to heaven. And then to her amazement, Mrs. Turpin saw a vast company of souls marching up that highway, including a "whole company of white trash . . . and battalions of freaks and lunatics shouting and clapping and leaping like frogs," along with people of color. And then she saw people like herself bringing up the rear, filled with "great dignity," attuned forever to "common sense and respectable behavior." And then, Ruby "could see by their shocked and altered faces that even their virtues were being burned away." What Ruby discovered was the unaccountable, upside-down favor God bestows on God's creation; especially on those who are often regarded with contempt by people like Mrs. Turpin. In a powerful spiritual revelation, Ruby sees that God favors and forgives by some standard that doesn't reflect Ruby's values. The vision gone, Ruby returns to her home, hearing the evening sounds, "but what she heard were the voices of the souls climbing upwards into the starry field and shouting hallelujah."[22]

Isn't this fiction? Yes, to be sure, but it's also a very faithful rendering of the teachings of Jesus about the place of the poor and disenfranchised in God's kingdom. In a strong sense, it's the very unexpected upside down of God's valuing humanity that Ruby finds so distressing and yet, at the same

21. O'Connor, *The Complete Stories of Flannery O'Connor*, 508.
22. O'Connor, *The Complete Stories of Flannery O'Connor*, 509.

time, remains true to the gospel. The last will be first, the wages of all the laborers paid the same and God through Christ will redeem them all, even the ones for which we as humanity cannot account.

The takeaways from this story are so rich, it's hard to know where to begin. But surely one point must be the nature of the full community of humanity in God's eyes. No matter how we would like to value ourselves as individuals and, as in Mrs. Turpin's case, largely assume the best of ourselves, we are part and parcel of the great company of diverse people, none better or worse than us. As the fifth chapter of James instructs,

> Listen, my beloved brothers and sisters. Has not God chosen the poor in the world to be rich in faith and to be heirs of the kingdom that he has promised to those who love him? But you have dishonored the poor. Is it not the rich who oppress you? Is it not they who drag you into court? Is it not they who blaspheme the excellent name that was invoked over you? You do well if you really fulfill the royal law according to the scripture, "You shall love your neighbor as yourself." But if you show partiality, you commit sin and are convicted by the law as transgressors. For whoever keeps the whole law but fails in one point has become accountable for all of it. (James 5:5–10, NRSV)

Pointedly, as far as Christians are concerned, we are in this world together, tied to one another and God by sacrificial love, what Christians call agape love. To be anything less than forgiving people fails the law of love.

There's a difference between Mrs. Turpin's judgment and God's. Ruby Turpin has a ladder-like scale to which she assigns people according to her perceptions of their value. She believes that she and Claude are located higher up, as befits her stern moral status. Lower are people of color and white trash, though Ruby's confused in her own mind where exactly they should be assigned. Ruby thinks she understands God's judgment, a judgment she believes that God shares with her. Even though Ruby's categorization of people is her own, she believes that God shares her views and that they are shared by most of humanity, including both Christian conservatives and liberals. Ruby and nearly all of us share an enculturated prejudicial justice. But God's judgment, as Ruby experienced in her pig pen epiphany, operates quite differently. God comes for everyone, absolutely everyone, and appears if anything to reverse Ruby's carefully contrived order. God has a different sense of order, a different standard of valuing community in mind. We welcome God's judgment because it's not prejudicial. God's judgment signals that God means to set the world right for every human being and God's creation.

The Old Order Amish and the Practiced Community of Forgiveness

On October 2, 2006, Charles Carl Roberts planned and carried out the murder of a group of Old Order Amish[23] girls at the Nickel Mines School, in Lancaster County, Pennsylvania. Roberts's plans included tying the girls and possibly assaulting them, having already sent all the boys running from their one-room school house. When Roberts threatened the girls, one of the girls cried "take me first." Suddenly, Roberts was interrupted by people arriving and he began to kill the girls. Five of them died and one of the girls was permanently injured. The slaughter was a horror story widely reported locally and nationally.

Sadly, news like this has become all too common. From terrorists to school massacres, to movie theater slaughters and high school revenge killings, such terrible violence has somehow been woven into a kind of cultural ordinary. What set the Nickel Mines School murders apart? As was widely reported, the Amish community not only immediately forgave Roberts but in fact came to his family's aid. On the day of Roberts's memorial, a sizable portion of the congregation was comprised of Old Order Amish, some of them victims of Roberts's violence.

Given our contemporary ideas about justice, punishment, and forgiveness, it's hard to account for this Amish communal forgiveness. Surely, we have heard wonderful stories of forgiveness from disparate places such as South Africa and East Los Angeles, but the Amish forgiveness was quite extraordinary. In this case, nearly the entire Amish community appeared to immediately, almost instinctively, forgive Roberts and in turn, sought to aid Roberts's family and their own community families with healing attention.

When the Amish response was reported in the national news, people reacted to the reports in many ways. Some pundits were filled with admiration, some with astonishment, and no few observers were filled with anger. The angry people wanted to know, how could the Amish possibly forgive such a heinous crime? Still others were angry because the Amish quick response to forgive appeared to minimize the crime and even absolve Roberts of the murders. Howsoever people responded to the reports, something

23. The Old Order Amish, an American term for Amish practices, maintain a particularly strict observance of their faith including a ban on phones and automobiles.

astonishing to the secular world had occurred—in a world bent on speedy justice, acts of reprisal, and judicial tit-for-tat punishment, the Nickel Mines Old Order Amish had committed to another path. The Amish had tapped some deep spiritual well of Christian faith to summon a forgiveness apparently rarely if ever seen or experienced in the world at large.

We are fortunate to have an accounting of the tragedy and its aftermath of forgiveness in a book written by Donald Kraybill, Steven Nolt, and David Weaver Zercher, entitled *Amish Grace: How Forgiveness Transcended Tragedy*.[24] If not for the authors' culturally sensitive and sympathetic reporting, it's hard to know how the communal narrative of forgiveness would have been told. The three authors took the time to discover how such graceful forgiveness was possible.

Their book deserves a fuller reading but I want to draw attention to the three authors' report of several elements of the community character that make the Old Order Amish forgiveness distinctive. The Old Order Amish are, as Christians say, not of the world but in the world. It's not that the Amish don't know about the world outside their communities or about the people they call "English." But the Old Order Amish have instead deliberately committed to live a particular style of life that reflects their commitment to the elements of their faith. In their fashion, they have echoed Paul's New Testament call for Christians to be in the world but not of the world. For example, despite the Amish well-known aversion to modern technology, some Amish do have phones on their farm (if their local church agrees) but in no case, would that phone be kept in the house where it could disrupt family time. The Amish don't have the notion they're more pious or better than others; instead they have realized that without a disciplined commitment to a manner of life that reflects their simple values of God and family first, they cannot be faithful in the way they wish. In short, the Amish way of living is the warp and weft of their faith.

Given the hand in glove of witness and way of life, I was surprised to discover that there's little formalized about the Old Order faith. Even so, there is a formalized and strong sense of an accountable community of practice. The Amish schools have an acronym they observe among what they call "scholars"—"JOY." "Jesus first, Others next, Yourself last." Such a phrase may well be anathema to some of the modern world but common standards of mutual practices like JOY help account for the young woman insisting to Roberts that he take her first. According to the Amish

24. Kraybill, Nolt, and Weaver-Zercher, *Amish Grace*.

community, the individualism that would reject JOY as anathema has become the great divide between them and the world. In a strong sense, the Amish young and old alike are immersed in the practices of their faith until those practices become an instinctive part of their individual characters. When you are accountable to everyone in your church, you'll soon discover that the hard work of forgiving even a murderer is much better done when you are surrounded by people committed to supporting and strengthening your practice of faith.

The stories held dear by the Amish descendants of the early Anabaptists help form their way of life. An early Anabaptist fled his would-be captors across an ice-covered river. When one of his pursuers fell through the ice, the Anabaptist returned to aid the fallen officer. Subsequently captured by his pursuers, the Anabaptist was put to death. As the authors of *Amish Grace* point out, the Amish don't have an independent doctrine but they do have stories that help them withstand "the acid test of secularism." When outsiders ask the Amish why they do what they do, they either point to the Bible, especially the Beatitudes and the Lord's Prayer, or tell stories like the above. With underpinnings like these, the Amish strengthen their resolve not to carry out retribution and to abhor violence.

As *Amish Grace* reports, forgiveness, nonresistance, and humility have become part of the fabric of Amish life. You cannot explore one of the qualities without respect to the others. I would note that the Amish commitment to nonviolence undermines the vengeful aspects of secular culture and from that, an aspect of the secular understanding of forgiveness. While secular forgiveness often includes judicial punishments, even when forgiveness is offered, the act of forgiveness entirely depends on the offender making lasting change. Forgiveness in the secular world is a human initiative. Not so in the Amish culture. In the most everyday way, all of the elements of Amish life are initiated by God, not by people. The Amish don't offer to pray for people as many in the secular world do. That would be too prideful and usurping the work of God. Instead they volunteer that they will keep people in their thoughts. God's initiative first, human initiative, follows.

We cannot exaggerate the centrality of mutual support and mutual accountability in the Amish community. Amish churches are purposefully kept small and regional to this end. Amish churches put JOY to work even in their worship, where no one person is more important than all the others. This understanding of community must be at least exotic if not alien to the secular world. To be clear, the Amish do recognize the therapeutic value of forgiveness. But they don't make the therapeutic value the condition for forgiveness. Instead they forgive because that's what people who follow Christ do. No one in the Nickel Mine tragedy was left to their own devices. Even if nothing was to be said (or could be said), the victims' fellow Amish would just come and sit with the victims and their families. They call it a "ministry of presence." Where contemporary secular culture, or even churches, might leave the comforting to professionals or select individuals, the Amish involved everyone in the work of compassion.

The authors of *Amish Grace* called the Amish "counter-cultural." That would be an appropriate expression in secular terms. But I suspect, if pressed, the Amish believe that they are following Christ, the true culture, indeed the true grace, offered to humanity. In other words, the Amish aren't counter-cultural, they are of the prime culture of the kingdom of God.

With that assertion, we have arrived at a critical juncture in our discussion of modern secular culture and Christian culture in the secular world. If you find yourself admiring the character and qualities of the Amish, why not adopt them and become practitioners of what I call their "instinctive" forgiveness? The answer lies in the long historical and cultural underpinnings of Anabaptist life. The Amish understand themselves be part of a narrative that extends from the time of Christ until now. Every part and parcel of the fabric of their lives reflects their deep spiritual convictions. Amish life has become literally a school for faith and nothing but faith. The thick recursive elements of their faith, humility, compassion, nonviolence, and an instinct for forgiveness are interwoven. You cannot practice one quality in full without the others. Pulling one thread will not unravel the blanket of faithful practices.

What then are Christians living in a thoroughly secular culture called to do? I can only think we are called to rebuild our communities anew, much as the communities of the Pauline world were called. We must come to see ourselves as first citizens of the kingdom of God and only then, participants in the secular world. Can this be done? I believe it can. We have examples of the New Monasticism here in the United States and in Great Britain where the Christian members have established religious communities of mutual support and mutual accountability. Members of these monastic communities become living examples of faithful presence. Other covenant communities, such as the Episcopal Worker Sisters of the Holy Spirit, have achieved mutual spiritual support while remaining committed to be living examples of Christ in the world. If we devote our imaginations, following God's indicative in the cross, the Beatitudes, and in the Lord's Prayer, we may well discover that we can become paragons of Christ's forgiveness.

7

Sin and Christ's Atonement

IF THERE ARE TWO traditional Christian terms that get less use in today's world than "sin" and "atonement," I would be hard pressed to say what they are. I made a casual survey of a few friends who preach regularly and I asked them to do a word search in their sermons for the words *sin* and *atonement*. I received several rueful replies to my email inquiry. Fewer than 25 percent had mentioned "sin" in a sermon and none had mentioned "atonement." Since both terms are intimately bound to the work of the cross, the hinge of time, and the center of the Christian hope, we must wonder why.

I remember when I first grew aware of the declining conversation about sin. As I wrote earlier, I was raised in an evangelical household—sin was mentioned often, especially in relation to our morals and salvation. But outside of home and church, I rarely heard about sin. I was in graduate school in the fall of 1973 when Karl Menninger's *Whatever Became of Sin* was published.[1] While the book achieved a level of popularity at the time, I remember that the faculty at my school regarded the book rather scornfully. Perhaps there were good reasons—after all, the soul-shattering Vietnam War was still raging and American appeared to have bigger problems—but I remember being struck by the evident lack of concern for talk about sin by my mentors.

Since that time, there have been any number of books, some of them well received, speaking of sin. When I turned to Amazon for the same sort of book and manuscript count that I made for the word "forgiveness," I found there were even more books and other publications that referred to

1. Menninger, *Whatever Became of Sin?*

sin or the seven deadly sins, some 17,000. Evidently people still care about sin, though I think we can agree that sin is rarely spoken of in polite company or in the popular media.[2] We may care about sin, even think about it, but we don't engage it in public dialogue. And if we don't discuss our ideas of sin with others, especially other Christians, our notions will often be stuck in the time where we first heard them.

There may be any number of reasons why sin gets so little play in our thinking; I should think that therapeutic thinking as it relates to human life plays a large part. On one side, we have the therapeutic approach that could well regard talk of sin to be inordinately negative and unproductive for mental health. We tend to think that people make mistakes, errors of judgment and the like, but wonder whether we should call these actions "sins." That seems unduly harsh. For some people when we talk about sin, it has the sense of something indelible, permanent by nature, and very prejudicial.

On the other hand, the moral relativism of our time, born of cultural pluralism, exposes the antiquated picture many contemporary people have of sin. Sin has come to be regarded either as discreet acts of wrongdoing or otherwise an arcane and dated picture of human nature. Usually, the emphasis falls heavily on individual acts of wrongdoing and even when we speak of sin and human nature, the evidence of sin in human nature seems hard to explain. Despite the desperate woes of the twentieth century, the terrors of Hitler, Stalin, and Pol Pot, some have been persuaded that humanity has come of age. We have arrived as fully capable people, products of our destiny and perfectibility. In truth, moderns have a very hard time talking about a human anthropology shaped by sin. The commonly held notion that we as humanity continue indefinitely into perfection flies in the face of talk about sin.

I believe we don't know how to talk about sin because we don't believe we have sinned. Indeed, and this is an axiom of Christian faith, we cannot talk about sin at all if we have not seen our shortcomings in light of the cross and the life of Christ. Paul made this clear in his letters—before we knew about the law, we could not have known of sin. Without the illuminating light of a God who seeks to restore the creation through the power of the cross, we can see no sin at work.

I take sin very seriously, especially sin as it's colored and shaped our communities. But at the same time, I do not think that sin defines what it

2. Note DeYoung, *Glittering Vices*, and Willimon, *Sinning Like a Christian*.

means to be human. I suspect that more than a few of the people who have no regard for religion, or who regard themselves as agnostic or atheists, are turned off by talk of sin. These people have perhaps rightly focused on the religious frauds who try to turn talk of sin to their own, often material, advantage. Send in twenty dollars and you will be assured a blessing! God created humanity not for sin but for love. I believe God primarily approaches us with grace and forgiveness, and not first with judgment of our sins. In God's eyes, we are not first and foremost sinners but instead first and foremost God's good creation. I come down on the side of James McClendon, who wrote in his book *Doctrine*, "We must not identify human being with sinful being; we must not erect the doctrine of sin into a barrier to goodness not even Christ can overcome; we must not be so serious about sin that we fail to be more serious still about grace."[3] McClendon makes the point that when we obsess over our burden of sin, not only do we fall short of divine qualities, we also fall short of what it means to be a "genuine" human being. Christ himself chose to be among us in human form. He hardly chose a form that would be alien to the promise of God's love and hope.

While many people regard sin as individual acts such as stealing a pen, arguing with a neighbor, or being angry with your spouse, some Christians have long regarded sin as more of a disposition than a collection of discrete acts. Paul regarded sin as a power alien to ourselves that can turn something made for our good, the Law of God, to a sinful advantage (Rom 4:13–15). Sin in Paul's sense may not only be something within us but something without us, a power that acts on us and subverts our best intentions.

What makes for sin if it's not a collection of discreet acts of wrongdoing? McClendon offers a simple definition: "Sin is whatever falls short of, whatever denies, whatever misses the way of faithfulness to God's rule embodied in Jesus Christ."[4] In sum, I think we could say that sin is everything antithetical to living like Christ. In an even stronger way, we could say that sin is the power of idolatry, a power that values things like privilege, power, and prestige above imitating Christ. Jesus Christ came preaching and teaching the kingdom of God, for this world and for the next. From the parables of Jesus, from his miracles, from his teaching, we gain a full picture of the hope of the kingdom. We even know how life will proceed in the kingdom because we have the Beatitudes to guide us. Ironically, it's not empty piety that leads us to imitate Christ ("The Sabbath was made for

3. McClendon, *Systematic Theology: Doctrine*, 135.

4. McClendon, *Systematic Theology: Doctrine*, 124.

humankind, not humankind for the Sabbath"—Mark 2:27) but instead the faithful following of Christ.

Remember how Jesus spoke to the woman caught in adultery. She was brought to Jesus so that she could be made an example. The religious authorities mean to stone her for breaking the law but Jesus tells them, "You who are without sin, cast the first stone" (John 8:1–11, NRSV). No one quibbles with Jesus about some abstract definition of what it means to be a sinner; instead, the authorities all go home, leaving the woman with Jesus. When Jesus asks the woman who is left to condemn her, she tells him no one. And then without her asking Jesus to do so, he refuses to condemn her and tells her not to sin again. Where's the judgment? Where's the punishment? Where's the moment of conversion? We can only take away the sense that sin does not make up the woman's nature but grace and forgiveness make up God's nature. If adultery stands between the woman and the better life of the kingdom, then stop living that way. Live as though other people and yourself matter deeply to God.

Robert Jenson has an even more simple explanation of sin. Jenson writes, "The only possible definition of sin is that it is what God does not want done." Jenson continues that in "history's entire tedious smorgasbord of sins presents only various ways of not being one thing, righteous."[5] We can see from earlier discussions that acts that might be regarded as sin in one culture may not be in another. Heaping up individual definitions of sin is self-defeating—instead, we need to find a way to live in this world as Christ lived in this world, not focusing on individual acts but instead on our disposition towards God and humanity. Humanity can be full and complete because we know Jesus Christ, fully human, was full and complete.

Paul saw sin as not only a power at work to subvert from inside humanity but equally from the outside. One of the problems with seeing sin as discreet acts of individuals is that we fail to take seriously the institutional or cultural power of sin. People are eager to absolve themselves of sin with regard to enculturated sins such as racism or economic oppression. In the minds of these people, if they as an individual have not committed the particular sin then nothing redounds to them. And yet, we know we are all part of a greater humanity. Even if we did not individually support an attack in South Sudan, or if we did not commit an atrocity against Palestinians, we can follow the steps that connect us economically or culturally to those atrocities. It's become commonplace to talk of "Six Degrees of Separation,"

5. Jenson, *Systematic Theology: The Triune God*, 133.

but indeed we are joined to the plight of the people of the Sudan and the West Bank by economic policies and attitudes of which we play a part, policies that are far fewer than six degrees away. The Sudanese suffer injustice with no hope of escaping through emigration and the Palestinians suffer illegal Israeli developments even while the US confers billions of dollars on that government. The sin may be seen from a distance but we are part of the economy, society, and government that contributes to the bellicose problems that dominate these people. This sin is not our intention, but as Haddon Willmer writes, "To see that the misery imposed on us is sin, the falling short of the glory of God, illumines what goes on in much of life, *where people are made sin against their intention and have to take responsibility for living what they do not approve of.*" (Italics mine) Willmer continues, "to be involved in the world, sometimes as beneficiary, sometimes as factotum, sometimes as a mere by-stander, is to be made sin, through what we have not chosen or caused."[6]

How does that sense of sin work? I heard Desmond Tutu tell a story about a time when he grew furiously angry with a young man who invoked hated rules of apartheid against him. The archbishop acknowledged that apartheid was a sin but in the moment, he suggested it was no lesser or greater sin than his self-righteous anger. For myself, I bridle at the economic oppression and military aggression in the West Bank, an oppression like a police state that takes critically needed water as hostage; I do small acts that I hope will help sustain hope, but I know that I am part of a larger order, government, and economy that benefits, however indirectly, from that oppression. I am made sin by a network of economic and cultural entanglements against my best intentions and desires.

This sense of sin sounds implacable and impossible to change. And that's where Christ's atoning work on the cross becomes so important. When we could not help ourselves, God came to our rescue through the cross and resurrection. The work of atonement gives humanity the opportunity to imagine a different outcome and a hope that that outcome will be fulfilled. To overcome the sense that we are determined to do evil even while we wish to do good (Rom 7:21–23).

6. Willmer, "Jesus Christ the Forgiven," 23.

How Atonement Sets Humanity Free

Why did Jesus have to die on the cross? And what did God and the Holy Spirit, the other two aspects of the Trinity, hope to achieve with his death and later resurrection? Such simple questions with such challenging answers. These questions have been answered in different ways in different eras of humankind. From the earliest centuries, people outside the church questioned how an ignominious death by a Roman method of capital punishment could possibly lead to salvation. And add to that, the claim that this human was also a God. Inconceivable. We can read in the Gospels and the New Testament literature that the authors struggled to make sense for their audience why Jesus had to suffer such a public humiliation and terrible death. For the first centuries of the church's life, Christians found themselves necessarily explaining the "why" of Jesus' especially painful and humiliating death. We know from the Gospels that Jesus thought it necessary to die in Jerusalem, which was the only place Jews could offer sacrifice. Jesus expected to be put to death as an innocent man, tortured and murdered by the powers of the day—the religious authorities who feared nothing less than the loss of their hegemony, and the Romans who brought their own violence to bear. The innocent God and man, refusing to employ the armies of the Divine at his disposal nor the entitlements due to him, chose the nonviolent path to lead the world to salvation.

Did that make sense? In the early decades of the church perhaps only to a few. Early on there were many derisive voices. The first image we have of Jesus on the cross was made by someone who derided the symbol by depicting the body of a man with the head of an ass. The graffitist wrote, "Alexamenos worships [his] God." You can understand the artist's mocking humor; how could such a contrarian action make sense, that a man subject to such terrible violence could die without resistance and yet in the process of dying and rising, conquer the universe?

The generations that have come and gone since that time have struggled to articulate the "why" and "how" within the cultural boundaries of their eras. For the first three or four centuries, no one theory of the atonement was ascendant over another. In fact, as Francis Young wrote, the very multiplicity of explanations served to support the rich complexity of work that God performed in the cross, where no one understanding necessarily denied the importance of another understanding. But Christians, like all who pursue the truth, are rarely comfortable in any age with multiple explanations—we seek to find a once-and-for-all explanation of just what it was that God did on the cross.

In the intervening centuries, there have been principally three ways that the church has described the work of the cross, three ways called "recapitulation," "substitution," and "moral influence." There's no need to get bogged down in lengthy explanations of the three but a brief review will help us. "Recapitulation" dates to the early centuries of the church. Looking through the lens of the early centuries, Christians who wondered why God in man would suffer so, contended that surely there must be a war between evil and good, between God and Satan, between two enormous powers, much like what the countries around them experienced. Christians wondered how they could explain why some people were so evil in the face of a loving God. The best answer appeared to be the notion that Satan by his powers had managed to capture humankind and hold them in bondage. How was God to restore these people to God? God acting slyly through God's son, using the Son as a kind of bait, slipped into the realm of Satan and set God's creation free through the cross. And why not? As James McClendon pointed out, didn't the palace intrigues of the time work the same way, where deception reigned and brought the regnant power the results they wanted?[7] If you see a problem with this explanation, you're not alone—the combination of a Satan who was nearly as powerful as God, and God's need to deceive to win humankind, caused no end of difficulties. A still better explanation was needed.

The Reformers presented another way to understand why Jesus had to die on the cross. Humankind was, by its own evidence, implicated in enormous evil and sin, so enormous that no human being could win a way out of the responsibility to make legal satisfaction, or in other words, pay the legal (sometimes penal) price for sin. God's law is God's law and even apparently, God cannot escape the necessary judicial calculation—someone must pay! Since humans had been brought low by their own sin, only God intervening for humanity through Jesus, both human and God, could pay the full satisfaction, that is satisfy the debt incurred by sin. Only God alone could repay God with the full reparation required by humanity's fallen nature.

Even though this theory of atonement remains regnant in some sectors, each reflecting its own cultural circumstances, there are problems. No few people in the West find repugnant the necessity of a blood sacrifice;

7. Cf. McClendon in *Doctrine.*

though that said, people in Third World countries, who see their suffering often written in blood, have fewer objections. The critical problem with the satisfaction theory appears to be that God must be constrained by rules that God created. In other words, God having created the law must abide by the law, where the law holds the superior influence. No surprise that people like Luther and Calvin (the latter with legal training) would arrive at this conclusion. Justice requires that reparations must be made! As Fleming Rutledge has made clear in her wonderful book, there's a long arc of God's justice from the Old Testament to the New, stretching to our time.[8] Someone must pay. And yet, without seeming capricious, can't God do what God wishes to do? Is God confined to the borders of God's own law?

There's one more aspect of atonement to consider—"moral influence." The trials of the past centuries, especially events like the Holocaust or the destruction of the atomic bomb, have shown us that humankind is far from perfect. Add to that the discovery in the last two centuries of the human psyche, a mind that can rebel against the very person who hosts that psyche, and we can arrive at a picture of humanity very much at odds with itself. As Paul wrote in the Letter to the Romans, we cannot seem to do the good we wish to do. We as humanity cannot seem to veer from our self-destructive path. The First World War and the trenches of the Somme dashed early twentieth century hopes that "man had come of age." We may not describe this brokenness as "original sin" though at the same time, we may wonder, "Why not?" In the view of moral influence, Jesus has come as the purest of human beings and by his evident self-sacrifice has shown us a better way—we can be fully the people God created us to be if we follow Christ through the cross. This purest of beings can by his very example shape the morality of our lives into Christian discipleship. Appealing though this sense of atonement may be, somehow it fails to take the objective experience of God's suffering seriously enough. God and man died on the cross to be raised. Moral influence was certainly implied but if God and man as one died on the cross, apparently more was at stake than morality.

However people seek to explain atonement, atonement is God's initiative to bring humanity to the fullness of God's creation. *The Oxford Dictionary of the Church* acknowledges that theories of atonement will no doubt continue to develop, reflecting the concerns of each age.[9] In other words, God has brought from the Trinity the best of humanity in Jesus.

8. Rutledge, *The Crucifixion.*
9. "Atonement," *The Oxford Dictionary of the Christian Church,* 122–124.

God has shown us in the life of Jesus' teaching, sacrifice, and resurrection that humanity can be in fact the marvel God created us to be. Whatever else we can say about atonement and forgiveness, we can say that God reached out to humanity through the creation of the Son to show that the kingdom life is not simply a good idea, but a way of life that can be lived simply, nonviolently, and with great sacrificial love.

One of the themes of our discussion of forgiveness is the "nonviolent" work of God in Jesus Christ. This nonviolence is not just an attribute of Jesus to mark in passing but an essential aspect of God's offering of forgiveness. God offers but does not compel, gives but doesn't force, and initiates forgiveness without God first requiring humanity achieving God's desires for them. What does all that signify? Apparently, it's beyond our human powers to know that we need salvation without Jesus first dying on the cross. To put the point plainly, much as Paul does in his letters, we have no way of knowing what we can be as loving human beings without Christ first dying and rising. To the point, we must be first saved by God to know we have fallen short of God's hope and ours. If it's true that we cannot learn to love without being first loved, then we cannot forgive without first being forgiven.

Does the priority of God's forgiveness seem to be out of order? Shouldn't humanity first admit their fault and then repent to be forgiven? We have been led to think that we must first acknowledge our sins, removing a barrier between God and us to achieve a full relationship with Christ. But as you can see in the work of the cross, in the initiative of the atonement, that is precisely the opposite of what occurs. We must first be forgiven in order to forgive; we must first be loved in order to love. Even mature Christians find it surprising that God has already completely forgiven our sins prior to any human initiative. If God's forgiveness had been partial or conditional, we could make an argument for a gradual approach to forgiveness and salvation. If conditional, we might have to satisfy this or that requirement and then be forgiven and saved. But God makes no prior requirements to God's forgiveness freely given. God in Christ and through the power of the Spirit steps into the middle of time and changes everything forever. All time flows towards the cross, the very center of our history of hope. All freedom and forgiveness flows out from that center.

Strand One was devoted to the human initiative of forgiveness, Strand Two, largely to the church's practice of forgiveness. Strand Three will be devoted to God's initiative of forgiveness, God's way of forgiving by God's forgiveness through Christ.

8

Strand Three: God's Radical Gift of Forgiveness

THREE STRANDS WOVEN TOGETHER to form the strong cable of forgiveness for our time. How are they interrelated? Each Strand is not only intertwined with the other Strands but the three are entwined in the culture of their time. No Strand exists without the culture it requires, including Strand Three, which requires the culture of the divine.

Strand One requires a culture of individualism to flourish. Strand Two could not exist without some form of community, especially the community of the church. That said, no larger community is required for forgiveness than the community of two, the offended and offender tied to one another by the offense. Questions about reconciliation, rehabilitation, and conversion, restoration, and justice require at least two parties. How would it be possible to be forgiven without first offending? Or to offend without someone to offend?

Strand Two emerges from the community's understanding of justice—the punishment needs to fit the crime and the community needs to first agree that the action is a crime. If there's a communal sense of crime, the crime needs be forgiven for social equanimity to be restored. Earlier, as we discovered in our discussion of atonement, even the work of the cross is understood by human minds located within a context, or culture, or an era within which we live. As an example, both the "satisfaction" theory and the "recapitulation" theory require an understanding of God that reflects a particular cultural or historical view. The satisfaction theory requires a largely legalistic, law-bound understanding of relationships. Even God must observe the law as if the law were a third and equal party in these relationships. As the people of the early and Reformation church reasoned, we have laws, apparently universal laws, and as a result, they must have come from God. The recapitulation theory requires a human view of a failed Adam restored in Jesus Christ. The early church questioned what could be a fit punishment for the "crime" of human idolatry and sin. They reasoned that the idolatrous sin of humanity requires the greatest price of all, God's self-offering in Christ on the cross. Nothing humanity has or could do could pay the price of restoring God's relationship with humanity; God alone could do that. When we move to our era, humanity more likely will view the moral influence theory of atonement as more useful and valid. Some are put off by the bloody and miraculous intervention of the cross and resurrection. Still others know that in this pluralistic world that laws in and of themselves are never universal or timeless. All we must do is examine our changing views on marriage or race to realize that there's no law so absolute or eternal that God too must abide by it.

If Strand One requires individualism and Strand Two community, what does Strand Three require? Strand Three requires Scripture, the story of God's work on our behalf and with God's work for us, God's essential freedom to be God. Unlike Strands One and Two, which can function entirely within the secular realm (even if both owe their origins to the Strand Three), Strand Three requires the radical freedom of God. God's radical freedom is shaped by God as Creator, who can exercise unconditional forgiveness because that God knows no physical, moral, or temporal contingency. God, unconstrained by anything but God, has entirely the freedom to radically forgive as God sees fit. That forgiveness likely will require us to modify our picture of how forgiveness functions in Strands One and Two. God can and does grant absolute and unconditional forgiveness according to God's purpose. Further, God forgives without reference to our human notions of justice and rightness. Does "unconditional" imply that God forgives all, universally? Are we as humanity expected to follow God's example?

Strands One and Two have been made problematic by the very culture that forms them. We see the world through the "lenses" our language and society have provided. We are unable to say that our image of the world and how we conceive it is fundamentally truthful and unblemished; how can we, as we live inside the very culture of which we speak? Anselm and Calvin, architects of some of our best atonement theology, were brilliant people, capable of extraordinary and lasting insights. But they too were a product of their times—even their greatest accomplishments were first built on the foundation of the cultures that formed them. We face the same issues. We live in a time where we have come to realize that lacking a universal and lasting definition, forgiveness has become to many people what Martha Nussbaum calls "transactional," that is, a representation of economic exchange much as we prize it in our communities. She wrote, "Speaking of forgiveness: Because our culture so reveres it, we shrink from examining it in a critical spirit. *Thus we may be slow, for example, to recognize elements of aggressiveness, control, and joylessness that lurk within it*"[1] (italics mine). Nussbaum continues, "we shall repeatedly observe . . . the tendency to use the word 'forgiveness' for whatever attitude one thinks good for the management of anger."[2] In other words, in our era we have turned to forgiveness for its utilitarian value, as a means to free ourselves of resentment or to manage the offended or the offender's anger. Strand Three reaches beyond the utility of forgiveness and the economic exchange Strands One and Two require. God, unconstrained by our ideas of a ruling economy, can grant forgiveness without us first paying the price.

Kathryn Tanner, in *The Economy of Grace*,[3] makes the point that we live in a contemporary society governed by the "exchange principle." "Tit for tat," trade one for another, we have come to believe that the lively exchange of one cost or debt for another has become the fundamental organizing principle of our world. The casual capitalist and everyday consumer rarely reflects on the fact that these economic principles have not always governed the human condition; they're not baked into God's design for us. In the Northwest United States, there is a historical Native American practice of the "potlatch," where the person gives away everything they own to their community to throw themselves on the tribe as a defining show of trust. Potlatch forms the economy of those many tribes with no suggestion of the sort of "transactional" attitudes Nussbaum writes about. No hint of capitalism emerges from that practice. Troubling though it may be to many, capitalism and its principles don't govern the order of the universe.

For an understanding of the essentials of Strand Three, let's turn to Scripture and the narrative arc of God's history with Israel and us. Jesus taught many things that defied the conventional wisdom and practices of

1. Nussbaum, *Anger and Forgiveness*, 58.
2. Nussbaum, *Anger and Forgiveness*, 59.
3. Tanner, *Economy of Grace*.

his day, especially economic practices. Of those I find Matthew 20:1–16 among the most intriguing:

> "For the kingdom of heaven is like a landowner who went out early in the morning to hire laborers for his vineyard. 2 After agreeing with the laborers for the usual daily wage, he sent them into his vineyard. 3 When he went out about nine o'clock, he saw others standing idle in the marketplace; 4 and he said to them, 'You also go into the vineyard, and I will pay you whatever is right.' So they went. 5 When he went out again about noon and about three o'clock, he did the same. 6 And about five o'clock he went out and found others standing around; and he said to them, 'Why are you standing here idle all day?' 7 They said to him, 'Because no one has hired us.' He said to them, 'You also go into the vineyard.' 8 When evening came, the owner of the vineyard said to his manager, 'Call the laborers and give them their pay, beginning with the last and then going to the first.' 9 When those hired about five o'clock came, each of them received the usual daily wage. 10 Now when the first came, they thought they would receive more; but each of them also received the usual daily wage. 11 And when they received it, they grumbled against the landowner, 12 saying, 'These last worked only one hour, and you have made them equal to us who have borne the burden of the day and the scorching heat.' 13 But he replied to one of them, 'Friend, I am doing you no wrong; did you not agree with me for the usual daily wage? 14 Take what belongs to you and go; I choose to give to this last the same as I give to you. 15 Am I not allowed to do what I choose with what belongs to me? Or are you envious because I am generous?' 16 So the last will be first, and the first will be last."

Many years ago, I was having dinner with a very successful businessman. The conversation turned to talking about the Bible passages that upended our perspectives on the world. The businessman averred that the Beatitudes, especially the verse "blessed are the peacemakers," was his greatest challenge. I asked him then about this parable from Matthew 20. He responded by saying he'd not heard it before. I took a moment to retell the parable. At that point, I was startled to discover that the businessman simple couldn't "hear" this parable! "Nonsense," he exclaimed, "Jesus couldn't have said something so patently ridiculous." Even when I took the Bible from my shelf and reread the passage, the businessman refused to believe that Jesus had told the story.

I'm sure this challenging parable has been conventionally interpreted as Jesus teaching about those who will come first and last among the disciples; whether we commit in faith to Christ in the beginning of our lives or at the very end, our reward will be the same. Fair enough. But let's change up the interpretation for a moment—what if Jesus also meant to recount how economics work in the kingdom of God, overturning all human expectations? What if indeed according to the economy of the kingdom everyone receives exactly the same wage at the end of time? And is it any great leap to conclude, following this parable, that when it comes to forgiveness, God doesn't repay, tit for tat, according to our sins? In fact, following the reading of this Gospel, God may forgive everyone, absolutely everyone, at the end of the day!

At my having suggested this unbounded forgiveness to people, some have responded to this notion of forgiveness without conditions as inconceivable just as my friend the businessman found the parable. "This simply cannot be!" And yet, I see no reason we cannot interpret the parable on its own terms; God, the creator of all that is and is to be, has perfect freedom to forgive by God's own standards. Why not, if you are God, find it possible to forgive everyone?

Is there an alternative to the "exchange principle"? Tanner believers there is, and it's called "giving." What if we thought of forgiveness as a gift? Are there unconditional gifts where we don't expect a full plate in return? Plainly there are, as almost all of us have given or received such a gift. The gifts may be as small as a neighbor clearing your walk after a snowstorm or as large as a secret donor paying your child's tuition. I have been often surprised in my life in the church at the number of large donors that want to remain anonymous—giving the gift was enough satisfaction for them. Tanner calls this "giving [as] completely disinterested, without self-concern, solely for the well-being or pleasure of others."[4] She continues: "Unconditional giving is not a matter of feeling or interior disposition but a social matter, an economic matter, a question of the way benefits are distributed to form social relations."[5] Tanner contends that as we conventionally consider gifts, we tend to think of them as gifts from the heart, manifestations of our feelings for the birthday person, the bride and groom, the spouse. But Tanner rightly points out that if a gift is given without expectation of return (as God might give), the gift upends the social formula. We cannot

4. Tanner, *Economy of Grace*, 57.
5. Tanner, *Economy of Grace*, 63.

owe in return for what was given unconditionally! Tanner concludes that the gift of "the cross saves us from the consequences of a debt economy in conflict with God's own economy of grace by canceling it." She continues that we are "snatched out of a world of deprivation and injustice from which now we suffer because of our own poverty, our inability to pay what others demand of us; and retuned to God's kingdom of unconditional giving."[6] Tanner's point seems almost too simple, that a gift can change everything. But what if indeed the gift was God's own self-giving of the love of the Trinity through the Son? What if the cross was the greatest gift of all? That's a gift for which no repayment could be made or be expected to be made.

If the "exchange principle" has become so culturally embedded as to obscure God's gift in the cross, what alternative understandings do we have? The French philosopher Vladimir Jankelevitch offers us means to think about forgiveness that might well open our eyes to other ways of thinking. Jankelevitch takes the pulse of modern forgiveness and he criticizes its function. He takes the arguably radical view that from the moment we start giving reasons why we should forgive "then forgiveness collapses back into something else such as excusing, clemency or reconciliation—none of which is forgiveness in and to itself."[7] Jankelevitch takes the view that forgiveness, in its truest sense, marvelously changes the relationship between the offender and the offended. That marvelous change is just that and only that—forgiveness. Forgetting, clemency, reconciliation in Jankelevitch's mind are not forgiveness. Jankelevitch believes that if we seek reconciliation through forgiving, then we have preferentially treated reconciliation, and the work of forgiving gets ameliorated.

I heard a theologian once say something similar that might illuminate Jankelevitch's view; the theologian contended that once we utter a sentence such as "God and justice," or "God and hope," employing the conjunction "and," that we have drawn limits around God's freedom to act among us. God is God and the actions of justice and hope are part and parcel of God, not "accessory acts" of God that God adopts from time to time.

While Jankelevitch does not count himself a theologian, he arrives at his philosophical view by a path that sounds theological. Whether we're the offended or the offender, he writes: "The will can do all—except one thing: undo that which has been done. *The power of undoing is of another order:*

---

6. Tanner, *Economy of Grace*, 65.

7 Jankelevitch, *Forgiveness*, xxi.

the order of grace if you will. It is a miracle"[8] (italics mine). As you can read, Jankelevitch's take on forgiveness shares our approach to the atonement. As humanity, we need the power of God's intervention through the cross, an intervention we call atonement, because we cannot change ourselves. The power of sin, whether within or without, holds us captive. In comparison, to Jankelevitch's mind, the power of the human will is just as limited, and we cannot finally change what's occurred no matter how we may desire that change. But grace can change the event, even if we must consider grace as a miracle.

Jankelevitch's take on forgiveness reminds us of divine forgiveness. Andrew Kelley writes of the philosopher that "[Jankelevitch] claims that true forgiveness alters the relationship between the victim and the wrong-doer. The victim no longer holds the misdeed against the wrongdoer, no longer demands any form of restitution from the wrongdoer, and renounces any claims to a moral advantage or high ground."[9] What you are hearing is a sense of absolute and unconditional forgiveness that I introduced earlier. God has the freedom and therefore the power to care for us as God wishes. Taking that forward, the prime definition of forgiveness that underwrites all other forms of forgiveness (including the secular individualism of Strand One) begins with both the absolute and the unconditional. If this sounds Platonic in its apparent perfection, perhaps it is. But I think Jankelevitch comes down on the side of the divine. In a very important way, he shows how absolute forgiveness precedes any notions we have of justice and rec-onciliation, of punishment and conversion, or of any other human function that places constraints on the why and how of human forgiveness. Clearly, divine forgiveness and human forgiveness share the term *forgiveness* but the latter, human sense is governed by human cultural limits and needs while divine forgiveness has miraculously no limits. Kelley writes of Jankelevitch that "if we forgive a wrongdoer simply to rehabilitate them then forgiveness is only the means of reconciliation or rehabilitation—if we are recognizing this is kiss and make up or that there are mitigating circumstances where we *don't need* forgiveness—we already have ways of dealing with these such as forgetting, reconciling, excusing and so on."[10] Jankelevitch's point makes a surprising claim, that forgiveness in its most important sense is nothing but forgiveness. Forgiveness is not reconciliation or forgetting but simply

8. Jankelevitch, *Forgiveness*, xx.

9. Jankelevitch, *Forgiveness*, xxiii.

10. Jankelevitch, *Forgiveness*, xxiii.

forgiveness and in that prime sense, does not require anything else from the offender.

Naturally, for people conditioned to a kind of transactional forgiveness, Jankelevitch's picture of forgiveness can be troubling. Returning to Tanner's point, our culturally conditioned proclivity is to demand some price from the offender. We expect what Nussbaum calls "payback." She goes on to say that "unconditional forgiveness in human relations is rarely free from some type of payback wish, at least at first."[11] But Jesus, fully human and divine, shows us another way: "the possibility is held out, then, of a love that is itself radical and unconditional, sweeping away both forgiveness and anger that is its occasion, a love that embarks upon an uncertain future with a generous spirit, rather than remaining rooted in the past."[12] Nussbaum hints at something boundless born of unconditional forgiveness, a love that's unconditional.

While such an absolute and unconstrained forgiveness might seem impossible, wouldn't it be fair to say that with God all things are possible? The initiative of the cross doesn't rely on the individual nor on the community or the church. The initiative lies with God who created heaven and earth and stands outside both of them as perfect love. When God broke into history through the power of the cross, God's gift of the Christ changed everything forever. Humanity didn't ask for Christ and the cross, though it's clear from Scriptures Old and New that we needed both. If what we must say about sin is true to sin, then we must also be blind to the evidence of our need. We were blind to the path of our own salvation. God knew what we needed and if we think of the cross as a perfect and complete act of forgiveness, then (following Jankelevitch), we can see that the atoning work of the cross miraculously changes our relationship with God. True, that change feels one-sided in the sense that God and God alone can initiate such radical forgiveness. But as the philosopher has written, if the desire simply for forgetting or for reconciliation is what God seeks for us, then we must respond as humanity within our own limitations. But if again, God has the absolute power to forgive, we humans, blinded by the power of sin, need do nothing to earn forgiveness—because by God's power, our relationship with God is miraculously transformed by God's grace. Truly extraordinary, don't you think?

11. Nussbaum, *Anger and Forgiveness*, 76.
12. Nussbaum, *Anger and Forgiveness*, 78.

Paul wrote in his letter to the Galatians: "There is no longer Jew or Greek, there is no longer slave or free, there is no longer male and female; for all of you are one in Christ Jesus" (Gal 3:28). All of us recognize in one fashion or another how radical Paul's claim is even by today's standards. But in the time of Paul, this claim would have been more radical yet. Writing to the Galatians, Paul's wrestled with the relationship between traditional Israel and the gospel to the Gentiles—how can they both be entitled to the good news of freedom? Notably, this claim to equal access to the gospel doesn't spring from Paul's own history; he is, by anyone's standards, the most educated and scrupulous of pharisaic observers. By his own history and cultural context, Paul should have militantly opposed this view. Just making the assertion that Jew and Greek share this same claim is radical enough, but to also include slave and free, male and female would have been beyond the pale of nearly everyone's experience. We need to discover how Paul arrived at this culture-shattering conclusion. When we do, we will peer even more deeply into a radical sense of forgiveness born of God's gift in Christ.

John Barclay in *Paul and the Gift* contends that as Paul sought to understand God's gift of Christ on the cross, Paul's faith-world shifted. Up until the time of Paul's conversion, Paul's faith traveled the rails of an urgent and demanding Judaism, known for its rigorous interpretation of the law. But following Paul's conversion, Paul came to see Christ and the cross as an unexpected gift not only to the Jews but also to the Gentiles. To be sure, the Jewish Paul surely expected a messiah but not yet, and not in terms of the cross and resurrection—not in terms of eternal life. Thus, Paul's encounter with the Christ event slashed the bonds of the expected entitlement of the Jews. Instead, as Barclay writes, "This incongruous gift bypasses and thus subverts pre-constituted systems of worth. It disregards previous forms of symbolic capital and thus enables the creation of new communities whose norms are reset by the Christ-gift itself."[13] To put that in plain language, the cross and resurrection dissolve all the expected entitlements and in doing so, dissolve all the preconceived cultural definitions including identity shaped by gender, culture, or economic status. By doing this mighty act, the gift of the cross "resets" all our cultural expectations and entitlements, opening the door to new kinds of community.

Barclay continues: "Paul thus identifies a divine initiative in the Christ-event that disregards taken-for-granted criteria of ethnicity, status,

13. Barclay, *Paul and the Gift*, 6.

knowledge, virtue, or gender."[14] What does this mean for us? Our cultural context is determinative of how our views and understanding of forgiveness proceeds. Strand One requires a therapeutic approach to initiate forgiveness, and Strand Two communal concepts of mutual justice initiate our shared forgiveness. But following Barclay and Paul, in Strand Three, God initiates forgiveness. God's "cultural context," being beyond our understanding, appears not to require a quid pro quo. Instead God's forgiveness comes as a gift and as such, not recognizing the requirement for any human appraisal of forgiving, undercuts and establishes a forgiveness beyond our human imaginings. And more than that, there appear no discernible boundaries or conditions to God's forgiveness as we discover it in the cross of Christ. Indeed, the cross came to us while we were yet enemies of God. Eugene Peterson's *The Message* makes this point in Romans 5:9–11:

> Now that we are set right with God by means of this sacrificial death, the consummate blood sacrifice, there is no longer a question of being at odds with God in any way. If, when we were at our worst, we were put on friendly terms with God by the sacrificial death of his Son, now that we're at our best, just think of how our lives will expand and deepen by means of his resurrection life! Now that we have actually received this amazing friendship with God, we are no longer content to simply say it in plodding prose. We sing and shout our praises to God through Jesus, the Messiah!

If God gave the gift of the cross without our asking, indeed without our even knowing we needed the gift, then as a gift God has put no prior requirements on humanity. The gift was given, as Tanner has shown us, and God has brought us to a world of "unconditional giving."

Stanley Hauerwas wrote of the conditions surrounding the unexpected gift and its effects in an article in *Soma*. "It seems Jesus does not understand that we, that is, we who assume modern accounts of responsibility, need to be forgiven only when we know what we have done."[15] Our discussions of Strands One and Two forgiveness require that either we recognize the need to forgive others or more commonly yet, that the offended and the offender agree on what the nature of the hurt may have been. But as Hauerwas points out, the gift of Christ on the cross actually illuminates our wrongmindedness. We didn't even know we were at odds with God until Christ came on the cross. Sure, we knew we had done individual acts that

14. Barclay, *Paul and the Gift*, 567.
15. Hauerwas, "'Father, Forgive Them.'"

were wrongminded, even perhaps sinful. But we were grievously unaware of how our dispositions alienated us from the God who created us from love and for love. Hauerwas points out that until the cross, we were unaware of "what kind of salvation we need. Through the cross of Christ, we are drawn into the mystery of the Trinity. This is God's work on our behalf. We are made members of a kingdom governed by a politics of forgiveness and redemption. The world is offered an alternative unimaginable by our sin-determined fantasies."[16]

We were unaware of "what kind of salvation we need." That doesn't mean that we as humanity did not know we needed salvation; no, in fact, as humanity has surveyed the twentieth century as the century of holocausts, from Auschwitz to Pol Pot, we recognize that we have fallen short of what we wished for humanity. But what the cross accomplished, we could not accomplish for ourselves—the cross incorporated us into the divine peace of the Trinity, offering us a way of living that we could not possibly have imagined without God's initiative. God alone can show us the deepest depths of forgiveness, of a forgiveness that has no conditions and no boundaries determined by ethnicity, economics, or caste. God has shown us a forgiveness beyond our human reckonings, beyond our ability to create ourselves, and given us hope and life.

One last question remains—does God expect us to forgive as God forgives? If Strands One and Two rely on human initiative, then the practice of forgiveness in Strand Three relies entirely on the initiative of God in Jesus Christ. God stands as the source of the unconditional and non-contingent forgiveness that God alone can give. Again, humans do not initiate unconditional forgiveness—but they may emulate it. God, who requires no economic or legal settlement, moral or character conversion prior to God's forgiveness, can literally remake the human community through forgiveness. God provides a way where we are neither Jew nor Greek, slave nor free, male nor female, but all beloved by God who's demonstrated that love through the cross. God absolutely and unconditionally forgives; can we be expected to do the same?

On first thought, we might be inclined to say "no," we cannot possibly forgive as God forgives. God is God and we are decidedly not God. But that said, we must consider again the case that God came for us not in fire or smoke, nor by angelic presence but in the form of a human being just like us. As we have seen, the atoning work of Christ depends on that interrelated nature of both divine and human. The human Christ, without sin or

16. Hauerwas, "'Father, Forgive Them.'"

any other fault, shows us what humans can be like. We are not Christ and while some spark of the divine may live in all of us, we are not the incarnation. The fact that Christ was fully human shows us something critical. If we wish to be like Christ, we can be perfected in every way. God did not set the bar so high that no human could ever attain it; Christ did live in perfection as a human being and as a human being, showed us what's possible for humanity. Many Christians absolve themselves of complete fidelity to the Christ life simply on the grounds that living like Christ would be "unrealistic." Much like the story of the laborers all being paid the same, we find it difficult as human beings to believe that God's actions, perfected in Christ, can be realistically attainable. But to treat God's way of life in Christ as impossibly unrealistic would also require that we abandon the hope of a way of life promised in the kingdom of God. God in three persons, the blessed Trinity, *is* reality. The Trinity's irenic relationship shows us how we are to live with one another. Every other effort on earth (remember the Tower of Babel, that parable of human cooperation seeking to be God only to go astray) to establish a lasting peace outside of the Trinity remains for Christians nothing more than a dark parody of that peace, and only leads to eventual failure.

And yet, God calls us to be disciples. The very term *disciples* indicates that we have much to learn. We are students of the greater good found in the cross and resurrection. We learn by imitation, following the Lord's example. That brings us to the final point, that while God does not expect us to be born from the womb in some absolute perfection of forgiveness, God does expect us to grow. Christians are disciples of the Living God. Just as we can get better at praying, reflecting, and worshipping, we can get better at forgiving. Can we be like Christ? If "like" means a sincere imitation with unbounded room for growth, yes, we can. We are expected to listen, reflect, imitate, and follow until we are gathered into the kingdom. We will be perfected into the body of Christ, the kingdom of God. Just as God initiates divine forgiveness, so too does God initiate our coming perfection in the kingdom of God. Perhaps the peace of the kingdom can only be known partially, but it's there for us to grasp, and the promise of the cross assures us that we will all one day fully know God's perfect forgiveness.

Some Remaining Questions

Very rarely have I had a conversation with people about forgiveness without hearing at some point, "What about self-forgiveness?" It's important to note that Jesus didn't bring up a concern for self-forgiveness in any of his teaching or preaching. That doesn't mean that Jesus did not care but it does mean that it's not a kind of forgiveness pursued in the first century. Perhaps that's a telling point, not only about how Jesus speaks of forgiveness, but also points to our changing historical perspective on forgiveness, an understanding that shifts with time and context. Despite that, there's enough concern with self-forgiveness in our time that we need to pay attention. No less a figure than Desmond Tutu urges us to self-forgive and to that point, I think we ought to consider how it works and how self-forgiveness relates to other forgiveness.

Earlier on, I pointed out how our present-day view of forgiveness must include both an offender and the offended; it's simple logic to see that at least two parties must be involved for both an offense and for the act of forgiveness. But that simple logic points up one of the problems with self-forgiveness, that is, that when we talk about the individual forgiving themselves, are we talking about two people residing within one person, both the offended and the offender? We know that at least since the era of Sigmund Freud that it's commonplace for us to think of our psyche in conflict with itself, parties such as the id, the ego, and the super ego clashing with one another for influence over the individual. Though some of Freud's work has been discredited with time, the paradigm of the individual at war with itself remains important in our time.

We don't have the space to review all the issues involved in the human psyche but the divided self has become such an important part of our cultural context that we can't simply set it aside. Never mind that the study of psychology plays little or no part in biblical times, psychology *is* a critical part of our time. When people talk about conflicting with themselves, we need to take that talk quite seriously.

When people speak of the need to forgive themselves, they're often speaking of those casual faults created by a slip of the tongue, simple thoughtlessness, or lack of attention. If talk of forgiveness helps us to deal with those evident human shortcomings, so be it. Every one of us trips over our own shortcomings at one time or another—why not speak of self-forgiveness as a step to simply accepting our failings and moving on?

There are however graver failings such as alcoholism, abuse, anger, adultery, and so on, failings far more serious than shortcomings. It's when we reflect on those failings that talk of self-forgiveness gets to be important. Let me suggest an approach that I think would be fruitful. Let's accept the insight that we as individuals can be so divided against ourselves that we can be self-destructive. But let's add as practitioners of Strand Three, God-initiated forgiveness, that when it comes to being God's created people, we are never alone. Even if we are of two or more minds within ourselves, God's never absent from that relationship. In a powerful way, that means that there cannot be just two entities within ourselves, but always three, the offended, the offender, and God. While I think it's sensible to talk about self-forgiveness given our current cultural context, I think it's even more sensible to think of self-forgiveness as a process whereby we remind ourselves that we are already forgiven. God by the power of the cross has already redeemed us from our failings; divided against ourselves almost to self-destruction, we can accept and embrace that forgiveness as being part of our psyche. Given the power of Strand Three thinking, I think it's perfectly appropriate to think in terms of self-forgiveness especially if that self-forgiveness includes the process of embracing the forgiveness that God has *already* given us. We're not perfect (though we are perfectible) and the God that has shaped us and loves us has already forgiven. Why shouldn't it follow then, that we can forgive ourselves?

The sense of God being ever present in forgiveness to God's creation, and humanity, can help us understand how it's possible to forgive the dead, those who are lost to us, and even those who refuse to forgive us in their self-righteous condemnation. Practicing Christians believe we don't live only within the context of our time, but much like Flannery O'Connor's Ruby Turpin, we also live within the illumination of eschatological time. God's promise of the kingdom doesn't only project forward into the resurrection, God's promise projects into our own time. Ruby's epiphany vision of the lame and halt preceding her into heaven changed Ruby's life not only for the time of resurrection but also for now. Ruby came to realize in her pig-parlor vision that the life of the kingdom of God begins now, that we need to learn to live the life of the kingdom now and not just in the promised future. Once we know the reality of God having already forgiven us, we live to a different scale of time. Just as Ruby discovered in her epiphany, we can discover that in the realm of the kingdom and in God's time, no one is beyond the reach of God's forgiveness and consequently, none then is beyond ours as well.

Many of us long to be free of our resentments, and further, be free to enjoy a community of friendship, forgiveness, and love. If we wish to be truly free, living the life of the kingdom even now, we must not only forgive seventy times seven times, we must also receive and embrace God's eternal forgiveness. When we do, we will grow free of our own divided spirits and free of the resentments that so darkly color our world.

9

A Brief Conclusion

I WROTE THIS AT the very beginning of the book and I would like to repeat it now: If you take nothing else away from this book, I hope that you will take away the faith that you're already forgiven. Our views of forgiveness will shift and change with time and context; it's difficult if not impossible to imagine how people will speak of forgiveness in another century or two. But if there's one timeless quality of forgiveness, not subject to the tidal forces of history and context, it's God's forgiveness that precedes even our knowing that we need to be forgiven. If the divine Creator who cares for us and loves us knew to forgive us even before we knew we needed forgiveness, perhaps it's time we should do the same for our fellow humanity. I can hardly think of a better form of evangelism for our time than that we witness to the healing power of Christ by forgiving one another. Our God came for us in the power of the cross so that we would know that nothing, absolutely nothing in the heavens above, in the earth below, or in the tectonic upheaval of human history can ever come between us and the power of God's forgiveness.

Bibliography

Arendt, Hannah. *The Human Condition*. Chicago: The University of Chicago Press, 1958.

"Atonement." In *The Oxford Dictionary of the Christian Church*, edited by E. A. Livingstone, 122–24. Oxford: Oxford University Press, 1997.

Barclay, John M. G. *Paul and the Gift*. Grand Rapids: Eerdmans, 2015.

Bromiley, Geoffrey, ed. *Theological Dictionary of the New Testament: Abridged in One Volume*. Grand Rapids: Eerdmans, 1985.

Bullock, Jeffrey L. *Practicing Christian Patience: Encouraging Community, Establishing Peace*. Harrisburg, PA: Morehouse, 2014.

Cavna, Michael. "Inside the mind of 'Inside Out': This is Pete Doctor's brain fresh off today's 2 Oscar noms." *Washington Post*. https://www.washingtonpost.com/news/comic-riffs/wp/2016/01/14/inside-the-mind-of-inside-out-this-is-pete-doctors-brain-fresh-off-todays-2-oscars-noms/?utm_term=9ae395537db1.

DeYoung, Rebecca Konyndyk. *Glittering Vices: A New Look at the Seven Deadly Sins and Their Remedies*. Grand Rapids: Brazos, 2009.

Dillistone, F. Wil. *The Christian Understanding of Atonement*. Digswell Place: James Nisbet and Co., 1967.

Franklin, Benjamin. *Autobiography*. http://www.thirteenvirtues.com.

Gopnik, Adam. "Why We Remember the Beatles and Forget So Much Else." *The New Yorker*, January 7, 2016. https://www.newyorker.com/news/daily-comment/why-we-remember-the-beatles-and-forget-so-much-else.

Hauerwas, Stanley. "'Father, Forgive Them.' A Leading Theologian Explores the Mystery of Jesus' Last Sayings." http://www.somareview.com/forgivethem.cfm.

Henderson, Michael. *No Enemy to Conquer: Forgiveness in an Unforgiving World*. Waco, TX: Baylor University Press, 2009.

Henning, Peter J. "White Collar Watch: Determining a Punishment that Fits the Crime." *New York Times*, November 7, 2016.

Hughes, Paul M., and Brandon Warmke. "Forgiveness." In *The Stanford Encyclopedia of Philosophy*, edited by Edward M. Zalta. https://plato.stanford.edu/archives/sum2017/entries/forgiveness.

Jankelevitch, Vladimir. *Forgiveness*. Translated by Andrew Kelley. Chicago: The University of Chicago Press, 2005.

Jenson, Robert W. *Systematic Theology: The Triune God*. New York: Oxford University Press, 1997.

———. *Systematic Theology: The Works of God*. New York: Oxford University Press, 1999.

Jones, L. Gregory. *Embodying Forgiveness: A Theological Analysis.* Grand Rapids: Eerdmans, 1995.

Konstan, David. *Before Forgiveness: The Origins of a Moral Idea.* Kindle ed. Cambridge: Cambridge University Press, 2010.

Kraybill, Donald B., Steven M. Nolt, and David L. Weaver-Zercher. *Amish Grace: How Forgiveness Transcended Tragedy.* Kindle ed. San Francisco: Jossey-Bass, 2010.

Levine, Amy-Jill. *Short Stories of Jesus: The Enigmatic Parables of a Controversial Rabbi.* New York: HarperOne, 2014.

Luskin, Fred. "Forgive for Good." LearningtoForgive.com, 2018. http://learningtoforgive. com/9-steps/.

Martin, James. "Brother Christian's Testament." *America,* November 14, 2015. https:// www.americamagazine.org/content/all-things/dom-christians-testament.

McClendon, James Wm., Jr. *Systematic Theology: Doctrine.* Nashville: Abingdon, 1994.

McFadyen, Alistair, and Marcel Sarot, eds. *Forgiveness and Truth: Explorations in Contemporary Theology.* Edinburgh, Scotland: T & T Clark, 2001.

Menninger, Karl A. *Whatever Became of Sin?* Stroud: Hawthorn, 1973.

Merritt, Jonathan. "Desmond Tutu's four steps to forgiving others: An RNS interview." https://www.democraticunderground.com/12644448.

———. "What Does It Take to Forgive Dylan Roof?" Religion News.com, June 22, 2015. http://religionnews.com/2015/06/22/what-does-it-take-to-forgive-someone-like-dylan-roof/#.

Musekura, Celestin, and Jones, L. Gregory. *Forgiving as We've Been Forgiven: Community Practices for Making Peace.* Downers Grove, IL: InterVarsity, 2010.

Nussbaum, Martha C. *Anger and Forgiveness: Resentment, Generosity and Justice.* New York: Oxford University Press, 2016.

O'Connor, Flannery. *The Complete Stories of Flannery O'Connor.* New York: Farrar, Straus and Giroux, 1971.

Rutledge, Fleming. *The Crucifixion: Understanding the Death of Jesus Christ.* Grand Rapids: Eerdmans, 2015.

Smith, James K. A. "The Justice of Memory, the Grace of Forgetting: A Conversation with Miroslav Volf." *Comment,* December 1, 2015. https://www.cardus.ca/comment/article/4739/the-justice-of-memory-the-grace-of-forgetting-a-conversation-with-miroslav-volf/.

Tanner, Kathryn. *Economy of Grace.* Minneapolis: Augsburg Fortress, 2005.

Taylor, Charles. *A Secular Age.* Cambridge, MA: The Belknap Press of Harvard University Press, 2007.

Tutu, Desmond, and Tutu, Mpho. *The Book of Forgiving: The Fourfold Path for Healing Ourselves and Our World.* New York: HarperOne, 2014.

Volf, Miroslav. *Exclusion and Embrace: A Theological Exploration of Identity, Otherness and Reconciliation.* Nashville: Abingdon, 1996.

———. *Free of Charge: Giving and Forgiving in a Culture Stripped of Grace.* Grand Rapids: Zondervan, 2005.

———. *The End of Memory: Remembering Rightly in a Violent World.* Grand Rapids: Eerdmans, 2006.

Willimon, William H. *Sinning Like a Christian: A New Look at the Seven Deadly Sins.* Nashville: Abingdon, 2013.

BIBLIOGRAPHY

Willmer, Haddon. "Jesus Christ the Forgiven: Christology, Atonement and Forgiveness."
In *Forgiveness and Truth: Explorations in Contemporary Theology*, edited by Alistair
McFadyen and Marcel Sarot, 15–29. Edinburgh: T & T Clark, 2001.

Young, Frances. *God's Presence: A Contemporary Recapitulation of Early Christianity*.
Cambridge: Cambridge University Press, 2013.